SHAKESPEARE'S COMEDIES
IN EASY READING VERSE

By the same author:

Shakespeare's Tragedies in Easy Reading Verse

Shakespeare's Histories & Romances in Easy Reading Verse

Shakespeare's Sonnets in Easy Reading Verse

Chaucer's Canterbury Tales in Easy Reading Verse

Charles Dickens' Oliver Twist in Easy Reading Verse

Charles Dickens' A Christmas Carol in Easy Reading Verse

Kenneth Grahame's The Wind in the Willows in Easy Reading Verse

SHAKESPEARE'S COMEDIES
in Easy Reading Verse

Richard Cuddington

Copyright © Richard Cuddington 2005
www.richardcuddington.com

The right of Richard Cuddington to be identified as the author of this work has been asserted by him in accordance with the Copyright, Designs and Patents Act 1988.

This book is copyright material and must not be copied, reproduced, transferred or publicly performed or used in any way except as specifically permitted in writing by the author, as allowed under the terms and conditions under which it was produced or as strictly permitted by applicable copyright law. Any unauthorised distribution or use of this text may be a direct infringement of the author's rights.

Cover design by Denis Grigorjuk
Illustrations by Michael Avery

Published by CompletelyNovel.com

ISBN 9781849149532

Contents

The Merry Wives of Windsor	2
Much Ado About Nothing	26
The Taming of the Shrew	60
The Two Gentlemen of Verona	86
The Comedy of Errors	116
The Merchant of Venice	154
Love's Labour's Lost	182
As You Like It	198
Twelfth Night	232
Troilus and Cressida	262
All's Well That Ends Well	278
Measure For Measure	306
A Midsummer Night's Dream	340

*Then finally he dragged himself
Up out and through the mud*

THE MERRY WIVES OF WINDSOR

Sir John Falstaff, old fat Jack –
Someone you maybe know –
Has just developed an idea
To make himself some dough.

He's short of ready funds and says,
'I think I'll have a bash
At carrying out a scheme I have
To make some ready cash.'

Of course he's no intention
Of working very hard;
This wouldn't suit old Jack at all,
That huge great lump of lard.

This lecherous and lazy knight,
This greedy, lying rogue
Smiled to himself and archly said
In his deep, winning brogue...

'I'll use my manly bluster
And all my crafty wiles
And good old Jack's most charming ways
And his most winning smiles...

'To prosecute a marvellous plan
That will ensure I get
A load of readies in my hands' –
And thus his scheme was set.

And so this stout old reprobate,
This reveller, this clown,
Proceeds upon his sneaky way
To good old Windsor town.

He'd pondered 'get rich' schemes before,
But now he thought, 'I'm blest!
For this one's quite a cracker,
One of my very best.'

He's come to Windsor with some friends,
For Mistress Quickly's there;
Both Nym and Pistol are with him
And they intend to share...

In all the fun and good old times
Their master always makes,
For he won't stop at anything –
He'll do just what it takes...

To entertain the ladies;
He'll have a drink or two;
Yes, anything that seems like fun
Is what this knight will do.

~ ~ ~

So Jack is now ensconced within
The noisy Garter Inn
And outlines his ambitious plan
Above the merry din.

He says, 'There's wives in Windsor,
I swear, that fancy me.
It doesn't take much working out
For me to clearly see...

'That Mrs Ford is really keen;
I'm sure she holds me dear.
I saw her gaze at me and give
A most "come hither" leer...

'Which truly made it very plain
Her heart was fit to melt,
For I could see in just a tick
How this poor woman felt.

'And Mrs Page examined me
In Windsor, yesterday,
Just like she was undressing me
In such a brazen way.

'And so I think I know for sure
What's on the lady's mind,
For I'm an expert on the needs
Of all of womankind.'

So this is Falstaff's clever plan –
What he decides to do:
'Both Mrs Ford and Mrs Page
I do intend to woo;

'For I have heard they both are wed
To men who each lay claim
To having massive fortunes so,
This now will be my game;

'I'll win the hearts of these two wives,
For I've been given word
They have free access to these funds –
At least that's what I've heard.'

What a devious, artful chap!
A villain to be sure;
Up for tricks that are within,
Or outside the law.

And now he plans to woo these two.
He really thinks he'll win
Their hearts and minds and their true love –
What world does he live in?

When was the last time that he looked
At his debauched old face,
Or down at his enormous gut
Which is a sad disgrace?

A long look in the mirror
Might just have made him think
That he was wasting all his time –
He'd give up in a wink...

All plans of winning their sweet hearts;
But no – poor sad old Jack
Thinks he's a handsome fellow as
He drinks his glass of sack.

And so he writes two letters;
Both missives are the same,
Except that he addresses them
With each a different name.

To Mrs Ford he'll send the one –
And one to Mrs Page.
But then old Falstaff gets into
A monumental rage.

For Nym and Pistol whom he asks
To carry these two notes,
Refuse to get involved and so
He grabs their scrawny throats.

But still this won't persuade them;
They say they just feel tired,
And so Jack Falstaff tells them both,
'The pair of you are fired!'

In anger and resentment then
Towards their boss, old Jack,
They both make up their minds to get
Revenge and pay him back.

So Pistol goes to Mr Ford –
He says, 'I've come to say
Sir John has sent a letter to
Your own sweet wife today.

'And in it he avows his love;
I swear upon my life
That Falstaff, that old scoundrel
Is set to have your wife.'

Now Ford was fiery in his way
And of a jealous turn,
So when he heard of this deceit
His rage began to burn.

And there and then, the fuming man
Vowed he would set a trap
To catch old Falstaff in the act.
He'd teach the cheeky chap!

Nym made his way to Mr Page
And to that worthy said,
'Falstaff is doing all he can
To get your wife in bed.'

But Mr Page laughed merrily
When of this plan he learned;
He trusted her implicitly,
So he was not concerned.

Then Ford and Page discussed it all
And both of them agreed
They wouldn't tell their wives they knew –
They saw no pressing need.

~ ~ ~

But as the husbands heard the news
The wives received word too,
Contained in Falstaff's letters which
Professed a love so true;

A passion burning in the heart
Of that conceited knight.
Heaven knows what all this meant!
It was a joke all right.

The ladies were astounded
When each of them compared
The letters filled with fervent words
That these epistles shared.

Contained within each letter,
To make the matter worse,
Were badly phrased and clumsy
Attempts at rhyming verse.

The ladies were amused, amazed –
And shocked – and both agreed
A lesson should be taught for this
Impertinent misdeed.

And they began to giggle as
They hatched a cunning plan
To have some laughs at the expense
Of this conceited man.

They said, 'We'll make the silly fool,
That fat old greasy knight,
Believe we find his drunken face
A very welcome sight.

'We'll make him think we love to see
His lovelorn, leering glances.
Yes, we'll convince the stupid ass
We yearn for his advances.

'We'll make him think his sodden face
Is welcome like the sun –
And thus, without a trace of doubt,
We'll really have some fun.'

One further thing they then agreed,
And that was not to tell
Their husbands what they planned to do,
Since Ford, for one, would yell...

And carry on in such a way
And let off so much steam
That he would very likely spoil
Their naughty, fun-filled scheme.

They went to Mistress Quickly and
Involved her in their plan;
They told her everything they had
In store for that fat man.

Then Mistress Quickly up and went –
As one of their accord –
To tell Sir John what time was best
To visit Mrs Ford.

'Her husband will be out when you
Have heard the clock strike ten.
Mrs Ford said, "Come to her,
And make your visit then."

'And by the way, my master dear,
I've also heard it said
That Mrs Page loves you as well,
You've really turned her head'

Well, foolish Falstaff beamed and thought,
'I am *the* man – by gad!
A gift to all the ladies fair,
A bold and handsome lad.'

So later on he made his way,
Dressed up like a lord,
Exuding charm and confidence,
To call on Mrs Ford.

The wives are waiting for him
And they have hatched a plan
That's guaranteed to make a fool
Of this absurd old man.

He knocks – and Mrs Page runs off
Within the house to hide,
While Mrs Ford, with welcome grin,
Now ushers him inside.

'Oh, sweet Sir John, why there you are,'
She gathers up her skirts
And says, 'Come in at once my dear.'
And brazenly she flirts.

He says, 'My heavenly jewel,
You're everything to me.
For you I'd cross a desert vast
Or swim across the sea.'

But Mrs Ford looks down, goes red,
And says, 'That's what you say,
But is it true what you profess?
Please answer this, I pray.'

She adds, 'You know, I think you love
That Mrs Page much more –
And thinking this has really cut
Your sweetheart to the core.'

'Oh, not at all,' the fat knight cried.
His voice was full of scorn.
'You are the only one for me.'
He tried to sound lovelorn.

'For I'm enraptured by your face,
Your lovely eyes, your hair.
That Mrs Page is plain and thin
And really can't compare...

'With you, my lovely Mrs Ford.
I couldn't love you more.'
But as he spoke a servant then
Appeared there at the door.

'Mrs Page is coming now,'
The servant loudly cried.
This was of course part of the plan
To take Jack for a ride.

He runs to hide as Mrs Page
Comes rushing in and cries,
'You're with Jack Falstaff, I'll be bound –
And don't go telling lies.'

Mrs Ford admits the truth;
(The girls are having fun.)
Then Mrs Page says, 'You'd best tell
John Falstaff there, to run...

'Because your husband's on his way –
He'll be here in a flash.
The best thing that Sir John can do
Is try to make a dash.'

But no – it really is too late:
That's what they tell Sir John.
The plan is going very well –
Of course, it's just a con.

So out of hiding Falstaff comes.
'Oh help me please,' he said.
'Your husband's sure to challenge me
And I might end up dead.'

'You'll have to hide,' the ladies cried.
'It's all there is to do.
Get in this laundry basket here.
We'll take good care of you.'

They stuffed him in the basket
With dirty pants and socks;
With greasy napkins, grubby ruffs,
Foul-smelling shirts and smocks.

What a profound indignity
For this vainglorious knight.
They said, 'It is imperative
That you keep out of sight.'

Once Falstaff was well hidden
With garments to his chin,
They fastened down the basket lid
And called some servants in.

Two men arrived and Mrs Ford
In shrieking voice then cried,
'Remove this smelly basket here.
Please take the thing outside...

'And throw it in the River Thames,
I'll have it here no more.'
Falstaff, in hiding, didn't hear
What fate he had in store.

And so the two men carried
The basket to the bank.
They threw it in the river, where
It very quickly sank.

Well, fat old Jack trapped there inside
Fought hard and pushed his way
Through dirty knickers, filthy rags,
And sheets all grimy grey...

Till finally his head popped out,
All soaking wet and cold.
He didn't look a valiant knight;
He just looked grey and old.

He spluttered, wheezed and coughed and sneezed,
He floundered, fought and blew
Great spouts of water from his mouth,
Tried every trick he knew…

To get his blubber and his bulk
Safe back onto the shore,
And as he did he shouted out
And cursed aloud and swore.

Then finally he dragged himself
Up out and through the mud;
Through slimy weed and clinging dirt,
Through all the muck and crud.

And standing on the bank he looked
Upon the dirty river,
Then turned his back and made his way –
Depressed and with a shiver…

Towards the Garter Inn, and there,
As soon as he got back,
He yelled out with a mighty roar,
'Bring me a quart of sack!'

Then once he had recovered,
He said, 'I tell you all,
I'll never cook up schemes again
Whatever may befall.

'I won't dream up these silly plans
In all my life again.
I never shall expose myself
To mockery and pain.

'I'm through with all this fooling,
Shan't do it anymore' –
But as he spoke Miss Quickly
Came striding through the door.

'Mrs Ford says she regrets
You wound up getting wet;
She says she'll make it up to you –
She'll make you love her yet.

'So, with apologies, she hopes
You now are feeling fine –
And will you come tomorrow
Sometime 'twixt eight and nine?'

Well, Falstaff sat bolt upright then.
He said, 'It's my old charm.
Yes, I'll be there you can be sure,
For it can do no harm.'

~ ~ ~

And so he makes his way again,
Now feeling reassured,
To see the lady he desired,
To call on Mrs Ford.

But when he gets there, he is told,
Just as he was before,
That Mrs Page is on her way –
But then there's worse in store.

For once again he hears that Ford –
Who fills him full of fear –
Is striding through old Windsor town
And even then draws near.

Mrs Ford cries, 'Hide again!
The basket's by the chair.'
Falstaff cries out desperately,
'I'll not get back in there.'

'Well, then we must disguise you.
Here put these garments on.'
When Falstaff looked he cried aloud,
'I really cannot don...

Habiliments like these – they are
A fat old woman's gear.'
But he was soon persuaded when
They said that Ford drew near.

The clothes belonged to some old dame
Who'd come from Brainford town,
And when she'd gone she'd left behind
This coloured, cotton gown.

The dress was huge, a perfect fit
For stout old Falstaff there,
But what he wasn't told was that
He really should beware...

For Mr Ford just couldn't stand
The Brainford woman, so
It would have been a useful thing
For poor old Jack to know.

While he was busy changing
Mr Ford came rushing in.
He thought that Falstaff might be there,
Committing carnal sin.

He grabbed the laundry basket –
Threw it across the floor;
He tossed the clothes around the room
And then he loudly swore...

That he believed Jack Falstaff
Was there to see his wife.
He said, 'If that old rogue is here,
I swear I'll take his life.'

But then an apparition
Comes waddling down the stairs,
And in a moment Mr Ford
Forgot his other cares.

The man was truly taken in.
He thought, 'That Brainford bitch!
I really hate her and I'm sure
That she's some kind of witch.'

He grabbed his heavy walking stick.
'I'll not have this,' he swore.
And with the most almighty blows
Drove Falstaff out the door.

Now after he had disappeared
The wives told everyone
About the scheme they'd put in place,
How they had had such fun...

Humiliating foolish Jack.
He'd got what he deserved.
'He is an ugly, silly man,'
Good Mrs Ford observed.

Her husband, now he'd heard the truth,
Remorsefully then said:
'I'm sorry I mistrusted you,
I must have lost my head.'

And then they all began to weave
Another devious plan,
To once again humiliate
That vain, flirtatious man.

They all agreed it would be fun
To have one final go
At making Falstaff look a fool,
Teach him a lesson – so...

They planned thus to entice the knight
To Windsor forest, where
There is a legend that says all
Should take the greatest care;

For dreadful 'Herne the Hunter',
Whom everybody fears,
From time to time, with ragged horns,
Within the wood appears.

He causes great destruction,
He runs and goes amok –
And here it is they plan to make
Sir John a laughing stock.

They gathered lots of children, and
To make them pretty scary,
They dressed each child to look just like
A nymph or woodland fairy.

They hope to make the bumptious knight
Quite frightened by this plan,
When all these fairies there accost
The unsuspecting man.

So Mistress Quickly goes to him
And says, 'The two good wives
Desire that you will come to them –
They love you with their lives.

'Please meet them in the forest glade,
They're waiting for you there.'
So daft Sir John sets off right then
With not the slightest care.

And they have asked that he dress up
As Herne the Hunter, so
He dons a hat with fearsome horns –
Oh, what a silly show!

He meets them and he's thinking,
'I've cracked it with this pair.'
But then a mighty crashing noise
Gives both the wives a scare.

They rush off into hiding;
The fairies then appear.
Falstaff crouches by a tree,
And trembles there with fear.

He watches as they dance around –
A sight he's never seen.
The man is truly terrified.
Whatever does this mean?

As he tries to hide he says,
'I hope they don't see me.'
But then one of the 'fairies' cries,
'Who's there behind that tree?'

They drag him out into the glade
And push and pull him round;
They pinch him and they punch him till
He falls onto the ground.

Tormenting him with mild abuse,
Some also burn his skin,
And then they twist and twirl him,
All in a dizzy spin.

They pluck some stems and with them write –
As Falstaff stands and blinks –
A motto saying, 'Evil comes
To him who evil thinks.'

They warn scared Falstaff then against
His sinful fantasy –
Of lustful and of shameful thoughts –
And he begins to see...

The error of his ways and how
He's really been quite bad;
That he has been a selfish knight,
A stupid, daft old cad.

And just as he was thinking,
'I can't take all this stuff,'
The folk who'd been in hiding
Felt he had had enough.

They stepped out from the forest
And stopped all the abuse;
They told the fairies to desist
And then they called a truce.

Sir John was very chastened
By all that had occurred,
And freely said he must have seemed
A creature most absurd...

For all the silly things he'd done.
He said, 'I've been so crass,
And I begin to see at last
I've acted like an ass.

'I am at your disposal
And so will thus fulfil
Whatever things you wish of me –
Please use me as you will.'

At this they all laughed heartily;
Page, who was standing there,
Said, 'Let's go back to my abode
Where all of us can share...

'A bottle of my finest sack.'
Jack Falstaff's eyes lit up.
He said, 'And will there also be
A chance for us to sup?'

Page laughed out loudly once again –
This was so like old Jack –
And then with glee he merrily
Clapped him across the back.

He said, 'And while you're at my house
There's one more thing you'll do,
For you can laugh there at my wife
Who right now laughs at you!'

*They left stunned Benedick behind
To ponder what he'd heard*

MUCH ADO ABOUT NOTHING

Much ado about nothing
Is the title of this ruse,
But don't be fooled dear reader
There's much here to amuse.

Our tale starts in Messina with
Two beautiful young girls,
Who we will come to know quite well
As our tale of love unfurls.

The first one was called Beatrice,
She was happy, light and gay.
Hero was the other –
Far more serious in her way.

They lived with Leonato
In a happy state of peace;
Shy Hero was his daughter,
Witty Beatrice his niece.

Leonato was the Governor
Of the lush lands all around,
And to his every whim and word
The peasants all were bound.

~ ~ ~

One day the girls on looking
From their upstairs window saw,
A troop of high born soldiers
Returning from a war.

Young and bold and handsome,
In war, they'd all fought well,
For each had acted bravely
And had a tale to tell.

Among them was Don Pedro,
Bold leader at their helm.
He was the Lord of Arragon,
A high prince of the realm.

And with him was young Claudio,
The prince's special friend,
And Benedick – known for his wit
That seemed to have no end.

All these courageous soldiers
Had visited before;
This had been some months ago
When on their way to war.

On arriving, they discussed
All that had happened since;
Benedick was speaking to
Leonato and the prince…

When Beatrice said to Benedick
In a sly, sarcastic way,
'Still talking then, though no-one heeds
A word you have to say?'

Benedick was most displeased,
This came from one so young.
He thought a well-bred lady
Should have a civil tongue.

He thought and then remembered
She'd made such jibes before,
And here she was now playing
These silly games once more.

'What then my Lady Beatrice
Canst be you're still alive?'
He looked at her with great disdain,
Indifference to contrive.

Now once again they argued
As they'd done in the past.
Their wit it bounded back and forth
Both furious and fast.

She said, 'I'll eat those you have killed
And do it just for fun.'
She said this to imply of course
He'd not killed anyone.

Allowing not a moment
To let her insult fester,
She added Benedick was just
The prince's unpaid jester.

He ignored her first insult.
He knew that he was brave,
For he had proved so many times
How a soldier should behave.

But when she called him jester,
'Twas the worst slur, forsooth,
A little near the knuckle,
A bit too close to the truth.

And so they verbally crossed swords.
Oh how the pair did carp,
For every word they uttered
Was mocking, mean and sharp.

And anybody listening
Would certainly have said,
That each would not have minded
To see the other dead.

For who could not be thus convinced
As all their scorn unfurled,
To think that each could not abide
The other in their world.

The prince, who saw them quarrelling –
To Leonato said,
'Oh what fun if we could get
That bickering pair to wed.'

He pointed to them saying,
'Would that not make you glad?'
Smiling, Leonato sighed,
'They'd drive each other mad.'

The prince replied, 'I do intend,
Now upon reflection,
To bring that warring pair into
A mountain of affection.

'For Benedick, I do believe
Would make an ideal spouse.
His honesty and valour would
Bring credit to your house.

'And I will show how we can give
Your Beatrice gentle shoves,
So she then vows that Benedick
Is the man she loves.

'And bringing them together
Will be our little gift.
Now come along with me and I
Will tell you of my drift.'

And though old Leonato thought
They'd only make bad weather,
The prince would not forsake his plan
To bring the two together.

~ ~ ~

Meanwhile Claudio had admired
Shy Hero from afar.
He thought she was quite lovely,
A bright and shining star.

And so he had addressed the prince –
He wanted him to know
How he adored fair Hero,
How much he loved her so.

The prince approved the match and asked
Her father to agree.
Leonato said, 'Of course,
'Twould bring great joy to me.'

So Claudio asked Hero
To be his dearest bride.
She said she'd be delighted
To spend life at his side.

Claudio wished to marry then
And do it in great style,
But he was told he must postpone
His wedding for a while.

He said to Leonato,
'My Lord, I truly say
Time moves along on crutches
Until love has its way.'

Old Leonato laughed and said,
'You must wait seven nights
Until you take my Hero –
Perform the marriage rites.'

The prince then said, 'Now Claudio –
I pray – don't shake your head,
The time will not pass dully
'Twixt now and when you're wed.'

And so to help to pass the time
For this impatient man,
The prince outlined the details of
His crafty, fun-filled plan.

His idea was the men would all
Make Benedick believe
That Beatrice was in love with him –
Oh what a web to weave!

Then Hero would get Beatrice
Worked up and in a stir,
And make her think that Benedick
Was now in love with her.

And hopefully this playful ruse
Would put an end to strife,
Beatrice would a husband gain –
And Benedick, a wife.

~ ~ ~

Thus Leonato and the prince
And Claudio as well,
Began to weave their devious scheme –
To cast their lover's spell.

For now they picked a moment
When Benedick was seated,
Alone among the garden walks
Where sometimes he retreated.

And as they walked along they kept
Out of Benedick's sight,
Deep in a conversation
That was casual and light.

Though Benedick could see them not,
Their dialogue was heard;
Eavesdropping from his hiding place
He heard their every word.

'Leonato,' said the prince,
'Now tell me – did you say
That Beatrice loved our Benedick
In a most passionate way?'

Said Claudio, 'I didn't think
That she could love a man.'
'Nor I,' said Leonato,
'But now it seems she can.

'For she now dotes on Benedick,
Who in the past she swore
Was someone whom she vowed with force
She loathed and did abhor.

'By my troth, my lord,' he said,
'I really do not know
What to think but truly now
It seems she loves him so.'

The prince then asked, 'And has she made
Her great affection known?
Has she informed good Benedick
How her true love has grown?'

'Oh no,' said Leonato,
'She swears she never will,
And this is torment to her
And makes her feel quite ill.'

Claudio said, 'Dear Hero says
It's always been her whim
To scorn him so she cannot now
Say she's in love with him.

'And Beatrice says she'll surely die
If he will love her not,
But die for sure if he should know
That she loves him a lot.

'And if he tried to woo her,
Well, she would always be
Full of her normal peevishness
And act bad-temperedly.'

The gentlemen now walked away;
They'd said their final word.
They left stunned Benedick behind
To ponder what he'd heard.

Now he had listened carefully,
'Can this be true?' said he.
'Can fiery Lady Beatrice
Be so in love with me?

'It's very hard to credit this.
She's always so aloof,
But if they're all convinced – well then
It surely is the truth.

'I never thought to marry
But now love has alighted,
The fervent love of Beatrice
Must surely be requited.

'For she is very virtuous
As any fool can see,
And truly wise in everything –
Save in her love for me.

'But hold – here comes good Beatrice;
I think I do espy
Her look of ardour shining bright,
And I know the reason why.'

She said, 'I've come against my will
To tell you, we're to dine.'
Benedick said, 'I thank you.'
As he looked for a sign;

Just anything that showed her love –
But there seemed nothing there.
Yet he was in no doubt at all
That really – she *did* care.

And though she answered tartly
And seemed quite out of reach,
He vowed he felt some kindliness
Beneath her sharp-tongued speech.

'There's double meaning in her words,'
He thought, 'This much I know,
That I will take great pains for her
And I *will* love her so.'

~ ~ ~

Now Benedick was fully snared,
He'd given his poor heart,
It then became young Hero's turn
To play a crucial part.

She sent for two young ladies
Who tended to her needs,
For both of them were loyal in
Their words and in their deeds.

'Good, sweet Margaret,' Hero said,
'Run to the parlour please;
Tell Beatrice to come look for me,
In the garden – by the trees.

'Tell her I am with Ursula –
To steal upon us there –
We'll be beneath the oaks and elms.
Tell her exactly where.

'Tell her she'll hear some secrets
She never will believe;
Things quite beyond her wildest dreams.
Things she could not conceive.'

Margaret did as she was bid;
Beatrice took the bait
And walked into the garden
Through the little gate.

On approaching she could hear
Them speaking of a man.
She wondered what it meant – of course
She knew not of the plan.

And so she hid and listened
And she heard Ursula say,
'Are you sure?' – then Hero said,
'I heard it yesterday.

'Claudio and the prince both said
That Benedick loves her well.
They asked me to acquaint her but
I said I'd never tell.

'I told them if they were his friends
They mustn't let her know.
If Beatrice knew he loved her – well,
How she would tease him so.

''Tis better that he live his life
Consumed with lover's sighs,
Wasting slowly inwardly,
Till finally he dies...

'Than die a death by mocking
And jibes with every breath,
For this would be a painful thing,
Like tickling to death.

'No, 'twould be best for Benedick
If he would somehow fashion
A life without sharp Beatrice
And quell his mounting passion.

'But what a pity, for except
For my own Claudio,
Benedick is the finest man
It's been my luck to know.'

And then they strolled upon their way
Leaving Beatrice agog,
For she could not believe she'd heard
This stunning dialogue.

'My ears are all on fire,' she cried.
'Can this be really true?
Farewell to scorn, contempt and pride.
I bid them all adieu.

'Oh dear Benedick, love on.
Best man in all the land.
I will requite your tender love,
Sealed with a wedding band.

'It's what they say that you deserve
And I believe they know,
So I will tame my racing heart
And I *will* make it so.'

~ ~ ~

And now we reach the part at which
You quickly will discern,
Our story is about to take
A most distressing turn.

The prince had a half brother
Who bore the title Don.
He was a nasty person and
Went by the name of John.

He loathed the prince, his brother;
His hatred knew no end,
And likewise hated Claudio
Who was the prince's friend.

He planned to stop the marriage –
He would take any measure –
His one and only reason being
For malicious pleasure.

Don John employed a villain,
Borachio was his name;
To ruin Hero's honour
Was their mean, artful game.

Borachio courted Margaret,
Sweet Hero's naïve maid.
Listen now most carefully
How this foul plot was laid.

He asked the simple Margaret
To go that very night,
To Hero's bedroom window
And stand there in the light.

To dress in Hero's clothes and thus
Enhance her normal style.
To meet with him alone and chat
And pass the time awhile.

Don John then spoke to Claudio
And the prince – and to them said,
'Young Hero flirts with strangers
While everyone's abed.

'The lady is disloyal
In every kind of way,
And will be even on this night
Before her wedding day.

'So come with me this evening;
You'll see what I have seen.
Come to her chamber window
And witness what I mean.'

Claudio said, 'I'll shame her.
I swear it on my life,
If I should find a reason why
She shouldn't be my wife.'

And so Don John accompanied them
At the appointed hour,
To wait and watch in hiding
Beneath fair Hero's bower.

There they beheld Borachio,
Which cut them to the core,
For with him was fair Hero –
That's what they *thought* they saw.

Of course it was young Margaret,
But in the dark of night,
'Twas easy to be taken in
And fooled by such dim light.

The shadows were deceiving;
The darkness all around
Made it very easy for
Confusion to abound.

A hundred times she bid him
A loving, warm goodnight.
The prince and Claudio beheld
This most unwelcome sight.

And as they looked they surely were
Completely taken in.
They were convinced that Hero had
Committed carnal sin.

Claudio felt an anger
That nothing would allay;
How *could* his Hero do this
Before their wedding day?

His love then turned to hatred –
He vowed he would besmirch
Her virtuous reputation
The following day in church.

~ ~ ~

Next day they all assembled
For the wedding – and the feast.
Young Claudio and his bride to be
Stood there before the priest.

His name was Friar Francis.
He said to Claudio,
'Wilt thou marry this fair lady?'
But Claudio cried, 'No!'

Then he accused shocked Hero
In the most fearful way.
'Why do you speak such words,' she cried,
'On this our wedding day?'

Claudio roared, 'She knows the heat
Of a luxurious bed.
'Tis guiltiness not modesty
That makes her blush bright red.

'So Leonato, take her back,
And sir, I beg, attend.
Give not that rotten orange
To me, your faithful friend.'

Leonato was perplexed.
'What do you mean, my lord?'
Claudio said, 'To marry not –
For it would be a fraud.

'I will not knit my soul unto
A loose and faithless maid.
Someone so foul and yet so fair –
Unto a wanton jade.'

Benedick was standing by.
He said – and earnestly,
'This seems not like a nuptial.
Well, leastways – not to me.'

Then Leonato asked the prince,
'Good sir, why speak not you?'
'Because the girl's not worthy.
What Claudio says is true.

'We saw her cheating,' said the prince.
'Such an unseemly sight;
Alone with a strange gentleman
And in the dead of night.'

At this poor Hero fainted
Upon the stone-flagged floor,
While Claudio and the angry prince
Strode coldly out the door.

Benedick and Beatrice knelt
Each side of Hero's head.
'Is she all right?' he asked her.
'I fear she's dead,' she said.

Now Beatrice would not entertain
A word of what she'd heard,
But poor old Leonato
Accepted every word.

He stooped beside his daughter.
Could hardly speak her name.
He was borne down with sorrow
And overpowering shame.

He cried out, 'Hero, do not live.
Don't open up your eyes.'
He cast around in agony
With tortured, mindless sighs.

'Oh how I loved and valued her,
And now to see her sink –
She's fallen with no hope at all
Into a pit of ink.

'And now the wide and endless sea
Can in no way contain
Sufficient drops to even try
To wash her clean again.'

But then the honest friar spoke out,
A clever man indeed.
Sharp were his observations
And merciful his creed.

He said, 'Hear me a little.
I've held my peace too long.
I have some words I'd like to say
Although they may be wrong.

'But as I've watched fair Hero
Colour up, then simply wilt,
These symptoms have convinced me that
She is quite free of guilt.'

He said to Leonato,
'Though this seems so appalling,
You can call me an old fool,
Ignore my age and calling...

'But I swear I've never seen
Such outright, blameless terror;
I'm certain that there's no guilt here
But just a shameful error.'

When Hero had recovered
The kind friar said to her,
'Who is this man they speak of?'
She said, 'I know not, sir.'

Then Hero said, 'Oh father.'
Her voice quite out of breath.
'If this is true then hate me
And have me put to death.'

The worthy friar spoke out again,
'There's much confusion here.
Young Claudio and his friend, the prince
Have got it wrong I fear.'

He turned to Leonato,
And with weary gaze then said,
'I think it best that for a while
We say poor Hero's dead.

'For Claudio and the prince just saw
Fair Hero faint away,
Thus they will easily believe
She died right here today.'

'However will this help, good friar?'
Fraught Leonato cried.
'What will become of all of this
If we say Hero's died?'

'Good will emerge,' the friar replied.
'Just put your trust in me.
Slander will to pity turn.
I'm sure that's what we'll see.

'When Claudio hears his love has died
I think that you will find,
Fond thoughts of Hero's sweetness
Will creep into his mind.'

Benedick remarked, 'He's right.
It is the thing to do.'
Leonato sighed – 'Oh well,
I'll leave it up to you.'

Then taking Hero by the hand
The friar led her away.
Benedick still with Beatrice
Scarce knew what he should say.

But then he boldly vowed outright
That Hero had been wronged.
To be cast with the dissolute
Was not where she belonged.

And then he felt quite overcome.
His ardent love unfurled.
He cried, 'I love no-one so much
As you – in all the world.'

Then Beatrice for her part as well,
No longer acting prim,
Declared, though it was very strange,
She loved no-one but him.

They hugged, their love now open –
They vowed to all above
That each was now forever
Committed and in love.

Then Beatrice said with feeling,
'Who'll right this wrong for me?
Who'll clear my dear, sweet Hero's name
For all the world to see?'

Benedick cried with passion,
'What would you have me do?
I'll do anything you want
To prove my love for you.

'Tell me what to do,' he begged.
(He was a man possessed).
'Kill Claudio!' she shouted.
Beatrice was most distressed.

'Not for the whole wide world,' said he.
His face blanched ghostly white.
He thought to kill young Claudio
Would really not be right.

'You kill me in denying me,'
Cried Beatrice, full of scorn.
Her words cut through bold Benedick
Just like a jagged thorn.

'Were I a man,' she cried, her voice
Was shaking in its pain,
'I'd see your fine friend Claudio
Was well and truly slain.

'What fancy words you do declaim.
What empty threats you make –
Oh for a man who'd help me right
This wrong for Hero's sake.

'All I see are men so full
Of selfish, proud deceiving.
Why can't I find a decent man
To ease a woman's grieving?'

'Enough then!' Benedick exclaimed.
'I'll challenge him for you.
Claudio shall pay the price
Before this day is through.'

~ ~ ~

Meanwhile poor Leonato
Thought his good name defiled
And challenged Claudio outright
For the honour of his child.

He cried, 'You've wronged my daughter,
You cruel, foul upstart.
And now we have to bury her;
Your slander pierced her heart.'

He said, 'Come sir – take up your sword
For I would run you through.'
'Nay, nay old man,' his foe replied.
'I will not fight with you.'

They argued back and forth awhile
Then Leonato left.
He was quite overcome with grief,
Borne down and so bereft.

Then angry Benedick appeared,
His sword clasped in his hand,
And boldly challenged Claudio,
'Draw sword and make a stand.'

But Claudio knew immediately
What must have happened here.
''Tis Beatrice has done this,' he said.
'Put you up to this, I fear.'

And yet he took the challenge
And would have fought his friend,
If something hadn't happened
To bring things to an end.

A constable came on the scene.
Dogberry was his name,
And he'd arrived to cast away
Fair Hero's unjust shame.

He strode with purpose and resolve,
Borachio at his side;
He told them how Borachio
And bad Don John had lied.

Borachio's conversation
By others had been heard.
He had condemned himself and John
With every nasty word.

For he'd been boasting to a friend –
As silly men will do –
When the watchman of the night,
Who had been out of view...

Overheard the awful wrong
He'd laid on sweet Hero.
And he'd gone to the constable
Intent to let him know.

His guilt was all too certain.
Transparent through and through.
He'd boasted of Don John's design
And what he'd made him do.

So he had been arrested
And brought to them that day.
Dogberry asked Borachio,
'What have you got to say?'

And so Borachio came clean
And freely did confess,
That he had been with Margaret
Who'd worn young Hero's dress.

He said that Margaret should remain
In everyone's esteem;
She was entirely innocent
And knew not of the scheme.

And any doubt that still remained
For anyone or other,
Was soon dispelled when news came in,
Don John had fled his brother.

Claudio was sorely grieved.
He wrung his hands and cried,
Because he'd wronged sweet Hero,
The lovely girl had died.

He spoke to Leonato.
His guilt was on display.
He wrestled with his words for he
Scarce knew what he should say.

He begged, 'Dear Leonato,
Forgive my wrong to you,
And any penance that you choose
I will most gladly do.

'Exact revenge in any form.
I'll do just what you bid.
I thought I spoke with truthfulness
When I said what I did.'

Leonato said with sadness,
'My daughter being dead,
You and dear Hero's cousin
Must now be wed instead.

'She is my brother's daughter,
And she is fair,' he sighed.
'Almost a living image
Of my poor child who's died.

'Let her take Hero's place and rights
Then I will not avenge.
Claudio – take her for your wife
And so dies my revenge.'

Claudio agreed to give
Leonato this relief.
He would do anything to ease
The father's awful grief.

He said, 'Oh good and noble sir
This does wring tears from me,
I'll gladly wed your precious niece
And faithful husband be.'

Claudio still loved Hero.
His heart was full of sorrow.
But he resolved to marry
This stranger on the morrow.

~ ~ ~

Next day the prince escorted
Young Claudio to his wedding;
An event, that truthfully
The poor, young man was dreading.

Leonato brought his niece.
She stood there at his side:
And Claudio bowed his noble head
To this, his second bride.

The lady wore a snowy veil
Of finest opaque lace,
To make quite sure that Claudio
Could not observe her face.

Claudio said, 'Fair lady,
Give me your hand I ask.'
'I will,' replied the stranger
And then removed her mask.

It was no stranger hidden
Behind the lacy mesh,
But Claudio's own dear Hero
Who stood there in the flesh.

Claudio saw that he had been
The victim of their lies,
But he was simply overjoyed –
Could not believe his eyes.

The prince asked, 'Is this Hero,
For she appears to thrive?'
'She died,' Leonato answered
'Whilst slander was alive.'

The friar said, 'We'll tell you how
We hid the girl away,
But not till this young couple
Have made their vows today.'

He was about to carry on
When Benedick up and said,
'I am in love with Beatrice –
We also wish to wed.'

So Benedick and Beatrice
Were married with their friends;
And with this great occasion
It's here our story ends.

Except to say that evil John
Was brought to book in time,
And hauled back to Messina
And punished for his crime.

And so they all lived happily
Once all of them were wed,
And thus it had been much ado
About nothing – as we said!

She had an awful temper

THE TAMING OF THE SHREW

Baptista lived in Padua
With both his daughters fair.
It was a lovely little town
And he liked living there.

Life should have been so easy –
But sometimes he felt harried
Because his darling daughters
Weren't settled down and married.

The youngest, called Bianca,
Had many suitors bid
For her hand – she really was
A lovely looking kid.

The older sister, Katharine
Was no such lovely dish,
She truly was a different
Kettleful of fish.

She had an awful temper
As everybody knew,
And she would never do a thing
That she was told to do.

Really quite unruly,
A problem to her dad,
He'd given up all hope that she
Would find herself a lad.

Because the long and short of it,
The whole truth – what the heck!
Was simply this – that Katharine was
A right pain in the neck.

And this was why she'd earned the name
That far and wide all knew,
Why she was known in Padua
As Katharine, the shrew.

Baptista now had made it plain
Bianca couldn't wed –
'No, not before your sister,'
Is what he'd always said.

So all Bianca's suitors
Were told to go away;
That it was just a waste of time
If they should choose to stay.

~ ~ ~

But then one day a bold, brash chap –
Petruchio by name –
Came bowling into Padua;
Wife-seeking was his game.

He didn't care what she was like
As long as she was rich;
He didn't care if she had not
The power to bewitch.

She could be ugly – horrible –
And really be a sight;
A toothless, awful sad old crone –
This still would be all right.

Money was the factor,
He didn't need a swan;
An overflowing dowry –
Well, that would turn him on.

Of Katharine's reputation
He'd been told – and to beware.
He said, 'I'm not too bothered;
I really couldn't care.'

He knew that she was very rich –
That was the crucial thing –
So he was quite determined
To give the girl a ring.

He was a cunning devil
And planned a devious game,
For he was sure that he knew how
To very quickly tame...

The wilful, wild, unruly girl
And teach her to behave.
He was without a trace of doubt
A very clever knave.

His normal character was calm,
Quite humorous and funny,
But he could cover this to win
A servile wife with money.

Once he had won her, then he planned
To act in such a way,
To make the crazy Katharine
Experience the dismay...

That she so often handed out.
He'd show his temper more
Than Katharine could – she wouldn't like
The moods he had in store.

For he'd take being awkward
To a whole new level.
He was intent to now act like
A far greater devil...

Than Katharine could ever be;
Oh, he would make her stew,
Till she became a loyal wife –
No longer Kate 'the shrew'.

Thus by these means he felt quite sure
That he could make her feel
Respect and love towards him,
And bring this shrew to heel.

He went to see Baptista,
'Look here,' he boldly said,
'I fancy your girl, Katharine.
I'd like for us to wed.'

Petruchio pretended that
He thought her meek and mild;
He didn't let Baptista know
He knew that she was wild.

Baptista though could clearly see
Petruchio was keen,
And being an honest fellow
He decently came clean.

He said, 'I'd like to see her wed –
Of this there is no doubt –
But I don't think you understand
What Katharine's all about.'

And he was just about to tell
Petruchio the truth
When Katharine's music teacher rushed
Right in and cried out 'Strewth!'

The girl had hit him with her lute,
And just for merely saying
He wasn't happy with the way
That Katharine had been playing.

And she'd called him a 'twanging twerp',
A 'rascal fiddler' too.
Her attitude had now confirmed
That all he'd heard was true.

Petruchio was not deterred
By what he clearly saw.
He said, 'She sounds a plucky lass;
I love her even more.

'So tell me, good Baptista,
What do I have to do
To gain your kind permission
To go to her and woo?

'You know I am not short of cash –
My father, who's now dead,
Has left me quite a fortune.'
He up and boldly said.

'So can you now inform me
What will her dowry be?
If I take Katharine off your hands
What will you give to me?'

Baptista found his manner blunt
But he had cash and lands
And was prepared to give some up
To get her off his hands.

'I'll give you twenty thousand crowns
And land when I should die.
I cannot offer more than that,'
He said with a deep sigh.

Petruchio was very pleased;
A deal was quickly done.
Petruchio would get the cash,
Baptista a new son...

And Katharine would be a bride!
Baptista went to tell
His daughter who, he felt quite sure
Would scream and storm and yell.

~ ~ ~

Now Petruchio began to mould
The outline of his plan.
He determined that he'd play
The even-tempered man.

For if she had a go at him
Or seemed as cold as ice,
He would pretend he found it all
Attractive, sweet and nice.

Or if she wouldn't speak to him,
He wouldn't take offence.
Instead he'd praise her loudly
For her fine eloquence.

And if she told him to be gone
He'd utter not a squeak;
He'd thank her just as if she'd asked
For him to stay a week.

When Katharine came into the room,
Petruchio said, 'Good Kate...'
But she replied, 'Don't call me that,
For it's a name I hate.

'My proper name is Katharine.'
Her wrath was clear to see.
'And that's how I must be addressed
If you would speak with me.'

'You lie,' Petruchio boldly said.
(A funny way to woo!)
'They call you bonny, pretty Kate –
And sometimes "Kate, the shrew".

'Because I've heard your mildness
Is praised in every town
I've come right here to woo you.'
Kate's face took on a frown.

They were left there on their own
And Katharine made it clear
Why men had been convinced that she
Was someone they should fear.

And while she raved and carried on
Like you have never heard,
He remained relaxed and cool
And praised her every word.

Then finally he said, 'Sweet Kate,
Don't make all this to-do,
For I am quite determined
That I will marry you.'

Just then Baptista came right back
And sly Petruchio said,
'Your daughter Kate has now agreed
The two of us can wed.'

But Kate denied this strongly;
She used the basest slang.
She said, 'I will not marry you;
I'd rather see you hang.'

She cried, 'How could I father, wed
A frightful brute like this?'
Petruchio lied, 'When on our own,
Why, we exchanged a kiss.'

He quite convinced Baptista that
Kate's love for him was true.
He said, 'She's merely putting on
This angry show for you.

'So give me now your hand, fair Kate.
To Venice I will go
To buy you fancy garments –
I'll be back before you know.

'We'll marry Sunday morning,
So kiss me, Kate – farewell.
Baptista please prepare a feast
And ring the wedding bell.'

~ ~ ~

When Sunday came one thing did not –
That was Petruchio.
Katharine cried, 'Why's he not here?'
They all said, 'We don't know.'

She wept from sheer vexation.
Called him 'a worthless cur'.
Had his proposal been a jest –
Just making fun of her?

She said then to her father,
'You forced me to agree,
But I am now convinced – quite sure –
We'll never ever see...

'That crazy con man here again;
He just tried to provoke
The notion that he wished to wed
But it was all a joke.'

Then suddenly the man appeared –
He burst into the room.
But he was not attired to be
A smart and proper groom.

His clothes were worn and dirty.
He seemed to bear the stamp
Of common, hard up working men –
He looked just like a tramp.

He wore old, tattered trousers;
Boots that didn't match;
A scruffy coat – he didn't look
To be much of a catch.

And his worn out, old servant –
Well, he too looked a mess;
And there was not the slightest sign
Of Katharine's promised dress.

They tried to get Petruchio
To change his scruffy gear,
But he just said to Katharine,
'It's me you wed, my dear.

'It's not my clothes you're marrying,
So don't make all this fuss.
Let's get ourselves into the church –
There's no more to discuss.'

The party headed off to church
On this the wedding day,
Petruchio just carrying on
In his eccentric way.

And when the priest stepped up and said,
'Is Kate to be your wife?'
Petruchio swore so loudly that
Astonishment ran rife.

Everyone was quite amazed –
It showed in every look.
The priest was so astounded that
He dropped his big, black book.

And as he stooped to pick it up,
Quite clearly in a huff,
Petruchio leant forward and
He gave the priest a cuff.

The poor man stumbled and his book
Again, fell to the floor.
Recovering the sacred tome,
The priest began once more.

And through it all Petruchio stamped
And swore and wore a sneer,
While Katharine stood there trembling –
The poor girl shook with fear.

Once he and Kate were married,
He said, 'Kiss me, now you're mine.'
Then in a raucous voice he yelled,
'Bring me a flask of wine.'

He deeply drank, then toasted
Everybody in the place;
And then he threw the glass's dregs
Right in the sexton's face.

He claimed the sexton's straggly beard
Was lank and grew too thin.
It was so drab and mangy
It showed his pasty skin.

He said this was his reason
For acting like a cad,
But he was just pretending
To be completely mad.

'Twas part and parcel of his scheme
(Though others had no clue)
To tame his wild, unruly wife,
Young Katharine, the shrew.

Baptista had prepared a feast –
It was a sumptuous spread.
Petruchio ignored it all;
'We're going home,' he said.

Baptista remonstrated;
The bride was angry too.
Petruchio would not be swayed
From what he wished to do.

'We're going now,' he loudly roared.
'My wife does what I say.'
And with those words he angrily
Dragged Katharine away.

He placed her on a scraggy horse
In such a sorry state,
The poor bedraggled creature
Could hardly take her weight.

As they travelled on their way
The only sound she heard
Were ravings from her husband and
She quaked at every word.

She was delighted to alight
Once they had reached his house,
But there was now much worse in store
For Katharine from her spouse.

For he'd made up his mind she'd not
Get anything to eat,
Or even get the chance to rest
Or ease her weary feet.

For when the servants laid a meal
With meat and veg and fish,
Petruchio took pains to find
Some fault with every dish.

He threw the food onto the floor.
He cried, 'Not good enough!
This will not do for you, my love.
You shall not eat this stuff.'

So Katharine went to bed at last,
Hungry and tired out.
But when Petruchio saw their bed
He raised his voice to shout.

'This bed is badly made,' he cried.
'The pillows are too hard.'
And then he threw the linen sheets
Straight out into the yard.

Katharine was shaken,
'I'll sleep in this chair,' she said.
Petruchio spent half the night
Just slagging off the bed.

He yelled about the servants, so
She didn't get much sleep,
And by the time the morning came
Poor Kate was fit to weep.

And then when breakfast was served up
Petruchio was the same:
Pretending to act kindly,
He played the selfsame game.

He said the food was rubbish and
To her despair once more
He threw each tasty morsel
Onto the parlour floor.

Petruchio at last went out
And stuck up, haughty Kate
Was forced to beg the servants for
Just *something* on a plate.

She pleaded with the servants,
'Some food – oh, I entreat,
For I am truly famished.
Bring me some thing to eat.'

But they said they didn't dare –
Their master would be sore.
She cried, 'But beggars get more food
Who knock at father's door.

'And here am I – I'm almost starved,
As tired as one can be.
And still my husband claims he acts
Just out of love for me.'

And then Petruchio returned.
He said, 'Look, I've brought you
Some meat that I have just prepared –
I've made a tasty stew.'

It was a tiny portion
But seemed a mighty treat,
Katharine was delighted that
She had some food to eat.

But before she'd finished it,
He took the food away.
He said, 'I can't allow my wife
To over-eat today.

'Besides, I've called the tailor
Who's made some lovely things:
Silken coats and caps and ruffs,
And here – some golden rings.

'And when you've tried them on, my dear,'
Exclaimed her loving spouse,
'We'll go and make a visit to
Your father's charming house.'

But this of course was all a sham.
Petruchio once more
Was playing with his hungry wife
Whom he *would* tame for sure.

For when she tried the garments on
He cried, 'Great heavens above!
You can't go out in clothes like that –
It wouldn't do, my love.'

He said, 'You can't call that a sleeve –
The thing's a total mess –
And I must say quite truthfully,
That is an awful dress.'

He drove the tailor from the room –
The man was duly paid.
Petruchio made quite sure he knew
He thought the dress well made.

This was all a further step
Along the road he planned.
And he'd informed the tailor
So he would understand.

Then to Kate he turned and said,
'We'll go and see your dad
Dressed in the clothes we're wearing –
They're really not that bad.'

Katharine didn't argue,
For she had given up.
She thought, 'At least at father's house,
I'll get a chance to sup.'

They left to see Baptista –
Kate had lost her wild ambition;
Her crazy spouse had beaten her
Into complete submission.

They met a man whilst travelling
Along a tree-lined glade;
Petruchio addressed him,
'Good morrow, gentle maid.'

Yes – he called him 'gentle maid.'
Was this some kind of joke?
Was he playing silly games ?
Just trying to provoke.

Well, he wished to ascertain
If he had tamed poor Kate,
If he had made her lose for good
Her every wilful trait.

Her spirit now was vanquished,
She had no will to fight;
She acted in a way to show
That all he said was right.

So she addressed the ancient man:
'It is so nice to meet
A young and lovely maiden,
So fair and fresh and sweet.'

The moment that she spoke these words
Petruchio up and said,
'Why how now, Kate – have you gone mad?
Have you quite lost your head?

'This is a wrinkled, withered man,
No maiden as you say.'
Then Kate replied, 'The sun's bright light
Has dazzled me today.

'I now can see that you're a man,'
She said with heavy sighs.
'Pray pardon me for my mistake –
The sun got in my eyes.'

So we can see, through loss of sleep
And lack of a good meal,
And by her husband's craziness,
How Kate was brought to heel.

'Good sire,' Petruchio then said,
'Where do you go today?
We'd love it if you'd come with us,
And help us on our way.'

The old man said, 'I'm travelling
To Padua – to my son,
For he is getting married,
For he has lately won...

'The hand of fair Bianca —
Baptista's girl, you know,
And he is called Lucentio,
And he is now her beau.'

The old man was Vincentio —
Petruchio knew his name —
And as their destination
Was going to be the same...

They travelled on together
To old Baptista's house,
Where young Lucentio then took
Bianca for his spouse.

Another pair had also wed —
Hortensio was the groom;
So all these happy people
Were gathered in one room.

The grooms were idly talking,
And then they made a joke
About Petruchio's sour wife,
And this is how they spoke:

They said, 'She's quite unbearable;
She's such a shrewish wife.
Her wilful disposition cuts
The air just like a knife.'

They said, 'We're very lucky to
Have wives who are so nice;
They're calm and easy going
And free from any vice.

'Petruchio has his work cut out.
A handful there – not half.'
They clapped each other on the back
And had a hearty laugh.

But after they had dined and when
The ladies all withdrew,
They started poking fun again,
They said, 'Your Kate's a shrew.'

Petruchio denied it.
He said, 'Let's set a test.
We'll have a little wager;
We'll have a little jest.

'We'll see which wife turns out the most
Obedient of all.
We'll see which one comes straight away
When she receives a call.'

The two new grooms agreed at once.
They saw no cause to fret;
They were convinced that they would win
So they proposed a bet.

'We'll wager twenty crowns,' they said.
Petruchio answered, 'No!
If we are going to have a bet
Let's bet some proper dough.

'Make it a hundred crowns,' he said.
So that's what they agreed.
Lucentio sent a servant to
Bianca, with all speed.

'Tell her to come here right away.'
Her answer struck him dumb;
The servant said, 'My mistress claims
She's too tied up to come.'

At once Hortensio spoke up.
He said, 'Entreat my wife.'
Petruchio said, 'I've never heard
Such rubbish in my life.'

The servant scurried off and then
Came back and said, 'Good sir,
She says you must be joking
And bids you come to her.'

So finally Petruchio spoke,
'Go to my wife,' says he.
'Command her presence here at once –
Tell her to come to me.'

The company all gasped aloud –
They were convinced as one
That fiery, headstrong Katharine
Would never ever come.

But lo! Within an instant
Katharine stood before her lord.
Astounded was the company –
It made them all applaud.

'What do you wish?' Kate meekly asked.
'What service can I do?
Anything you want, my lord,
That I will do for you.'

'The wives of these good gentlemen,
Go fetch them,' he replied.
'Their wilful disobedience
I really can't abide.'

So Katharine went to get them –
And shortly brought them back.
Petruchio said, 'Now you shall see
What your two women lack.'

And with the ladies standing there
Petruchio said, 'Now Kate,
You teach them good behaviour
And how to treat their mate.'

So Katharine told the sullen girls,
Quite of her own accord,
How they should treat their husbands;
Their duty to their lord.

Thus it was clear to one and all,
Petruchio, by skill,
Had now entirely taught his wife
To gladly do his will.

It really was amazing,
But clear for all to see
That Kate was now as dutiful
As any wife could be.

And she became the fairest wife
That all in Padua knew,
No longer disobedient and
No longer called 'the shrew'!

*Valentine would raise his eyes
Unto the heavens above*

THE TWO GENTLEMEN OF VERONA

A long time in the distant past,
You may say 'way back when',
There lived in fair Verona
Two noble gentlemen.

The first one was called Valentine,
And Proteus, the other;
Their friendship was so close and true
Each felt he had a brother.

Now Proteus loved a lady
Called Julia, and she
Was really quite as lovely
As any girl could be.

Proteus would speak of love,
'It's great,' he'd say, 'oh my!'
But on this subject these two friends
Could not see eye to eye.

For Valentine had no-one, so
When Proteus spoke of love
Valentine would raise his eyes
Unto the heavens above.

The more that Proteus spoke about
Fair Julia, his passion,
The more that Valentine would tease
For speaking in this fashion.

He said, 'My freedom's better
Than tortured love, my friend.
Your lovelorn life appears to cause
You heartache without end.'

Then Valentine one day spoke out:
'Milan's the place,' he said.
'I've had Verona up to here;
This town is really dead.

'For if a young man stays at home,
I'm certain that he'll find
He'll end up quite dull-witted
And with a narrow mind.

'If you did not love Julia
In the way you do,
I'd ask you to accompany me –
It would be good for you!

'But stay and may love thrive and grow
Each and every day.'
'Farewell, my friend,' said Proteus.
'I'll miss you while away.'

～ ～ ～

Valentine left for Milan;
Once he was out of sight,
Proteus took up pen and ink
And he began to write.

He wrote to fairest Julia,
To promote his suit;
He hoped that in her heart sweet thoughts
Of love would soon take root.

For though she loved him deeply with
A love that was as true
As his for her, she'd never said
The words, 'I love you too.'

She was a noble lady
And thought it for the best
To keep the hand of cards she held
Concealed, close to her chest.

So Proteus wrote his letter
With hopes he would persuade
The lady to return his love,
Then gave it to her maid.

She took it to her mistress,
Who gave the note no heed.
She said, 'It's not the kind of thing
I'd ever want to read.'

She told the maid, Lucetta, 'Go –
And take the letter too.'
But really it was not the thing
She wanted her to do.

She didn't want her maid to know
She'd felt sweet Cupid's dart
And that the handsome Proteus
Had stolen her poor heart.

And yet she wished to read the note,
So called her maid once more.
Lucetta came into the room
As she had done before.

'Now what's the time?' asked Julia.
Her maid thought, 'There's no way
My mistress really cares at all
About the time of day.'

She offered her the letter,
But Julia lost her cool;
She said she didn't want a note
From some poor, lovesick fool.

She said, 'Don't you presume to guess
What my true wishes are.
You are a very cheeky maid –
Too impudent by far.'

She grabbed the letter crumpling it,
And making lots of creases,
And then she tore the paper up
Into little pieces.

And as Lucetta made her way
Towards the chamber door
So Julia took the paper scraps
And threw them on the floor.

Lucetta went to pick them up
And sighed a passive sigh,
But Julia said, 'Get out of here,
Just let the paper lie.'

Once Lucetta had retired
Her mistress felt much better,
For now she was completely free
To gather up the letter.

On studying the fragments
The words that first she read,
Were these: 'Love wounded Proteus.'
'Oh, bless his heart,' she said.

Lamenting all his loving words
She'd thrown upon the floor
She wrote a kinder letter
Than any sent before.

When Proteus received it
He truly was delighted,
For here was indication that
His love might be requited.

'Oh, lovely Julia!' he exclaimed.
'To think you really care...'
But then his father came along.
He said, 'What have you there?'

'A note from Valentine,' he lied.
'Let's see,' his father said.
'Come let me read his latest news.'
But Proteus shook his head.

'He hasn't much to say,' he sighed,
'Though he's a lucky man,
For he has been befriended by
The grand Duke of Milan.

'He says how much he wishes
I was in Milan as well.
It all sounds quite exciting
From what he has to tell.'

His father said, 'Would you not like
To go there and to spend
Some time at that distinguished court
And be there with your friend?'

'My duty lies,' said Proteus,
Trying his best to hide
The true emotions that he felt –
'To be here at your side.'

His father had been chatting to
A friend who'd said to him,
'Why do you let your son stay here
Indulging every whim?

'For most young men go travelling,
They venture far and wide;
It's very strange that Proteus
Remains here by your side.

'And look! His good friend Valentine
Is at Milan's great Court –
Just think of all the benefits
And lessons he'll be taught.

'I am surprised that you allow
Your son to wallow here,
For it will do him little good –
Could ruin him I fear.'

So now whilst speaking to his son
The friend's wise words came back;
He felt his friend's opinion had
Been on the proper track.

He said, 'You say that Valentine
Would like you in Milan;
I think he's right – it would transform
A boy into a man.

'With your good friend I quite agree,
So to Milan you'll go.'
Proteus saw immediately
That he could not say no.

His father always got his way.
He sighed an earnest sigh;
He blamed himself for this result
Because he'd told a lie.

He'd been untruthful to his dad,
So now he must depart
And leave the maiden there behind
Who'd stolen his true heart.

When Julia heard the awful news,
Reserve flew out the door;
She soon stopped playing hard to get
And very quickly swore...

Her everlasting love for him,
And then both vowed those things
That every lover promises;
Then they exchanged gold rings.

~ ~ ~

Proteus soon left for Milan
And on arriving there
He found that his friend Valentine
Was now the one to care.

He'd fallen for fair Silvia,
She loved him madly too;
But it was all a secret,
So no-one else there knew.

She was the duke's own daughter,
The centre of his life,
But he'd made up his mind she'd be
Someone else's wife.

To Valentine the duke had shown
Great friendship from the start,
But he would not allow the lad
To claim his daughter's heart.

For he was quite determined
She'd marry Thurio,
And Valentine would never do,
Although she loved him so.

But Silvia hated Thurio,
Despite his ardent pleas,
For he had none of Valentine's
Appealing qualities.

The day that Proteus arrived
Valentine was engaged
In making fun of Thurio
And getting him enraged.

And they were both with Silvia
When the duke came in to say,
'Behold your good friend Proteus
Has turned up here today.'

Valentine was overjoyed.
He said, 'My lord, his face
Has such an air of nobleness,
His manner has such grace.'

'Then welcome him,' the duke replied.
'He's come here seeking you.
Now greet your good friend Proteus –
And with no more ado.'

Proteus strode into the room,
All bluster and good cheer;
Valentine said happily,
'It's good to see you here.'

He turned to Silvia and said,
'Meet Proteus, sweet dove.'
And Proteus, on meeting her,
Fell instantly in love.

When later they left Silvia,
A laughing Proteus said,
'So tell me how you're now in love;
Whatever turned your head?'

Said Valentine, 'I must admit,
I'm now of your accord,
For love has won – and humbled me –
He is a mighty lord.'

Proteus laughed to hear his friend
Admit his change of view,
But he was an unworthy knave
In what he planned to do.

He thought, 'I am determined now
To make fair Silvia mine.'
He would throw over Julia and
Betray good Valentine.

Then Valentine explained to him
And trustingly revealed,
How the duke was in the dark
And how they had concealed...

The passion that they truly shared –
How it was only known
To Silvia and to himself,
The two of them alone.

'The duke would never, ever let
His darling daughter wed
Someone who's not high-born – like me,'
With sorrow he then said.

'The duke intends that Silvia
Shall marry Thurio,
So we are planning to elope –
But no-one else must know.

'Tonight when everyone's retired
And safe and sound in bed,
Sweet Silvia and I will steal
To Mantua,' he said.

He showed his friend a ladder
Made from the strongest rope:
'This will be the vehicle
By which we will elope.

'She'll hang it from her window
Upon this very night,
And once she's climbed down safely
We'll disappear from sight.'

It's hard to credit such a thing
But in that hour, forsooth,
Proteus thought he'd go and tell
Silvia's dad the truth.

So he sought out the worthy duke –
Engaged him in a chat;
And after idle banter – well,
He slyly told him that...

He felt he should inform him
Of news that he had heard.
He told him of the lover's plan –
Repeated every word.

He said, 'Though I betray a friend
I really can't conceal
What Valentine is planning,
I feel I must reveal...

'His scheme to steal your daughter,
For you've been kind to me;
I feel it is my duty –
I can't just let things be.'

He told him, 'Valentine intends
A sly and cunning stroke,
For he's concealed a ladder
Beneath his heavy cloak.'

The duke then said to Proteus,
'If this is all the truth,
Then you're a most upstanding man,
A decent, honest youth.'

So when the duke saw Valentine
All wrapped up in his cloak –
Concealing his rope ladder –
The duke to him thus spoke:

'Where are you rushing to, good sir,
At such a frantic pace?'
Sly Valentine then stopped and said,
'Excuse me please, your grace...

'I have letters to deliver.'
This was of course untrue.
The duke said, 'They can wait awhile,
I would have words with you.

'Please tarry for a moment,
And put aside your mail.'
Then he began an artful ruse,
By telling him this tale.

He said, 'I have decided that
I must disown my child,
For she's become unruly,
Disrespectful, brash and wild.

'She will not marry Thurio
Although this is my wish,
So I will serve my Silvia up
A most unwelcome dish.

'From here on in, she's on her own,
I'll make her leave my house –
Her beauty and her grace alone
Must gain for her a spouse.

'Once this is done, I do intend
To find myself a wife;
In fact there is someone with whom
I'd like to share my life.

'But I'm right out of practice;
I don't know how to woo.
So I was hoping that you'd help
And tell me what to do.'

So Valentine then gave advice
On what to do to court;
He gave the duke in detail
The knowledge that he sought.

'But there is still a problem,'
The duke went on, 'You see,
Her father keeps her guarded,
She's under lock and key.

'I cannot get to see her –
There really is no way
That I can get to visit her
At any time of day.'

'Then go at night,' said Valentine.
'Be sure to take with you,
Some rope so you can scale the wall –
That is the thing to do.

'And on your way conceal the rope
Beneath a cloak like mine,
And you will see that everything
Will all turn out just fine.'

'Oh, let me borrow your fine cloak,'
The duke with passion cried.
And then he grabbed at Valentine's
And threw it open wide.

And there he saw the ladder.
'So what's all this?' he said.
And in the cloak he saw a note
From Silvia, which read:

'My Valentine, I'll wait for you
Upon this very night.'
On reading this the troubled duke
Turned pale – he went quite white.

He angrily told Valentine
How base and false he'd been.
He said, 'To steal my daughter thus
Would be extremely mean.'

He banished Valentine from court.
He said, 'I'll make it plain –
Don't ever try to see or speak
To Silvia again.'

~ ~ ~

Valentine then left Milan,
But just where could he go?
He knew his family back home
Would not want to know.

While he was wandering through a wood
A mile outside Milan,
About as low as he could get –
A lonely, banished man...

Some robbers jumped upon him.
They said, 'Your cash, my lad.'
He told them that the clothes he wore
Were truly all he had.

He said, 'I'm but a banished man;
My whole life's in a mess.'
They quickly saw he told the truth
From his immense distress.

And they could also tell at once
From his most noble air
That he was just the answer to
A humble robber's prayer.

They said, 'We need a leader.
There's a post here to be filled –
And if you don't accept the job,
We're sorry, you'll be killed.'

Valentine no longer cared
What would become of him,
And so he thought he might as well
Indulge the robber's whim.

So noble Valentine, who'd been
So well behaved and good,
Became the outlaw's leader,
Like England's Robin Hood.

~ ~ ~

But meanwhile what of Julia?
Well, she was wont to cry
Because her darling Proteus
No longer dwelt close by.

So she resolved to seek him out
By going to Milan,
And on the road, for safety's sake
She dressed up as a man.

Her maid, Lucetta, went as well,
Dressed in the selfsame way,
And when they reached Milan they found
An inn in which to stay.

The landlord spoke to Julia
And, with a pleasant smile,
Said, 'Would you like to come and hear
Some music for a while?

'The music has been organised
By a man tonight
To serenade a lady fair –
It should be quite a sight.'

Alas! A frown crossed Julia's face.
The reason was you see,
She thought, 'If I see Proteus
He'll be upset with me.

'He'll think I am no lady;
He'll think I'm much too bold.
My coming to Milan for him
Will turn his passion cold.'

But then she realised that if
She came within his sight,
As she was dressed up as a man
'Twould likely be all right.

He wouldn't recognise her,
Of this she was quite sure,
For she looked very different from
The way she had before.

Only if he scrutinised
Very carefully,
Would he then become aware
The *he* was really s*he*.

And so she said she'd go along
To hear the serenade,
So hurried off with her new host
And with her faithful maid.

They to the ducal palace went,
And, walking through the door,
Proteus declaiming love
Was what the trio saw.

He vowed he loved sweet Silvia,
But Julia heard her say
He was a naughty fellow
For speaking in this way.

'What of your true love, Julia?'
Silvia said with passion,
'And how could you treat Valentine
In this disloyal fashion?'

She slammed her window on him,
She said she'd hear no more;
His base, unfaithful conduct
Shook her to the core.

For she still loved young Valentine –
Her love just knew no end.
How could sly Proteus act like this
Towards his once good friend?

And Julia was most upset –
She flew into a rage.
Then she contrived that she'd become
Her faithless lover's page.

He'd parted with a servant
So had a vacancy,
So Julia thought, 'That post will prove
The ideal one for me.'

And this was all made easy
By Julia's cunning ploy
Of dressing up, to make herself
Look like a handsome boy.

Proteus offered her a job,
Commanding, 'Do one thing,
Go to Silvia for me
And give her this gold ring.'

She saw it was the selfsame ring
She gave him when he left!
This action now made Julia
Feel totally bereft.

But when she went to Silvia
She was relieved to find
The lady that her Proteus loved
Was really very kind.

Fair Silvia said, 'I do not want
Proteus or his love;
For I once heard that he adored
His Julia way above...

'All other women in the world.
Now he discards her – so
He's really not the type of man
That I would want to know.'

Julia said, 'I'm pleased to find
Your actions are so true...
I feel I should reveal the fact
That I know Julia too.'

She then spoke highly of herself –
As you'd expect she would.
She said, 'This Julia is fair,
Respected, sweet and good.

'She's just about as pretty
As eyes could ever see.
And truthfully I must admit
She looks a bit like me.'

Then Julia offered her the ring,
And Silvia cried, 'The cur!
That's Julia's ring – for he said once
It had belonged to her.'

And so fair Silvia's kindliness
Began to make a start
To cure poor Julia's sadness,
And ease her broken heart.

~ ~ ~

Silvia still loved Valentine –
This I think we know –
So she was quite determined
Not to marry Thurio.

So she decided she would leave
For Mantua – she'd heard
That Valentine was hiding there;
At least that was the word.

But he was with the robbers
And now inspired a fashion
For thieves to treat their victims
With kindness and compassion.

Silvia left for Mantua,
And Eglamour went too –
An old man to protect her, but
In truth, what could he do?

For when a robber stopped them
As they traversed the wood
Eglamour just ran away –
So *he* was not much good.

The robber saw that Silvia
Was truly terrified:
She shook with fear from head to toe,
Her eyes stared open wide.

'Be not afraid,' he gently said,
So Silvia felt relief;
'For I will take you now to meet
My new, fair-minded chief.'

But then her fear returned anew,
She thought, 'Oh dear! Poor me!
Valentine – my dearest love –
I suffer this for thee.'

Then as the robber took her
To meet his chief close by,
Silvia caught a movement
With her sharp-sighted eye.

It was unfaithful Proteus
With Julia at his side,
Still in the costume of a page –
Her own true self to hide.

For he had followed Silvia
And now, without delay,
Proteus fought the robber off
And sent him on his way,

And as he'd saved fair Silvia –
Given the thief the boot –
Proteus once more set out
To press his lover's suit.

Julia stood there silently
As Proteus urged his case.
She wore a solemn, anxious look
Upon her woeful face.

She thought that this courageous act
Of saving Silvia's life,
Would mean for sure, that Proteus
Gained Silvia for his wife.

But as she stood there watching these
Events she so much feared,
Silvia's true love, Valentine,
Quite suddenly appeared.

Appraised of Silvia's presence
And all that had occurred,
He'd come at once, with every haste,
To check on what he'd heard.

And there he found sly Proteus,
His former faithful friend,
Declaring love for Silvia
He vowed would have no end.

Then Proteus saw Valentine
And, seized with great remorse,
Apologised that he had let
His actions take this course.

Valentine was very kind –
To such a great degree,
That he informed his selfish friend,
'I shall set Silvia free.

'All my loving interest
I gladly give to you.'
It was a quite astounding thing
For Valentine to do;

And Julia on hearing this
Could not believe her ears,
For it confirmed the very worst
Of all her lovelorn fears.

Thinking Proteus would accept
She fainted on the ground –
But after a few moments
She started coming round.

Proteus eyed her closely.
'Well, bless my soul!' he said.
'It is my lovely Julia
Unless I'm off my head.'

He saw her love for him still burned –
It was extremely plain;
And this – her care and constancy –
Brought *his* love back again.

He dropped upon one knee and begged,
'Let's make a brand new start.'
She said, 'Oh yes, my Proteus,
With all my loving heart.'

So now that they were reconciled
Good Valentine then swore
Eternal love for Silvia
And said, 'Be mine, once more.'

But at that very moment
When love had won the day,
The duke and silly Thurio
Came passing by that way.

'We have been pursuing
Our Silvia,' they cried.
For Thurio still wanted her
To be his loving bride.

And so he grabbed sweet Silvia,
'This maid is mine,' he said.
Valentine replied, 'Stand back
Or you will end up dead.

'If you so much as touch her
You will breathe your final breath.
If you don't heed my words, right now
I'll bring about your death.'

Thurio was a coward.
He said, 'I'll tell you what:
Only a fool would fight a duel
For one who loves him not.'

The duke then said to Thurio,
'The fact that you won't fight
Shows me you're not a man at all,
So get out of my sight.

'I applaud you, Valentine.
You've proved to heaven above
And also to myself, that you
Deserve my daughter's love.'

Valentine then thanked the duke
And gravely kissed his hand,
And then he asked for clemency
For all his robber band.

He said that really, by and large,
Their crimes were very small.
The duke replied he'd pardon them,
The whole band one and all.

Then Proteus was forced to tell
Exactly how he'd been
As false a friend as anyone
Had really ever seen.

But once he had apologised
To all his faithful friends,
It was agreed by everyone
He'd truly made amends.

So to Milan they all returned
And there the good duke said,
'We'll have a celebration
And you can all get wed.'

So with this happy outcome
Our little intrigue ends;
Verona's two young gentlemen
Once more became best friends.

*'We watched the stricken ship drive on
And break up on a rock'*

THE COMEDY OF ERRORS

There long had been a quarrel
Between two famous states,
For each of them was riddled with
All kinds of fears and hates.

Syracuse and Ephesus
Are what these states were called;
Their quarrel would make any man
Really quite appalled.

For Ephesus had passed a law
Which made it very plain
That anyone from Syracuse
Would certainly be slain...

If they were found in Ephesus –
It's what the law decreed,
And there was only one sure way
The person could be freed.

That was by handing over
A lot of cash you see;
A thousand marks, it was the sum
To set intruders free.

It really was an awful law,
And what amazing cheek!
A way of making piles of cash
And bullying the meek.

~ ~ ~

It chanced one day a merchant
From Syracuse, of course,
Was found to be in Ephesus –
They dragged him from his horse.

The man was called Egeon;
A crowd of rough, course men
With violent hands got hold of him
And took him there and then...

To see the Duke of Ephesus.
They cried out with a sneer,
'Look here, great duke, upon this wretch,
Just see what we've got here.'

These common folk loved all such sport,
How they enjoyed these larks.
'Come on, you low-down merchant man,
We want a thousand marks!

'Or by the law you'll surely die.
Hand over cash, you swine.'
But there was just no way that he
Could ever pay the fine.

The duke said Egeon must pay
Or else he'd have to die.
'But ere you do, you must relate –
You really must tell why...

'You travelled here to Ephesus;
A stupid thing to do.
You knew if you were captured here
'Twould mean the end of you.'

Egeon sighed a weary sigh;
He said, 'My life's been tough,
And I don't care if I'm to die
For I have had enough.

'You tell me to recount my life,
The worst thing you could ask;
Reliving all my sorry woes
Is not a pleasant task.'

But then Egeon told his tale.
He said, 'It may amuse
And while away some time for you –
It starts in Syracuse.

'For there it was that I was born.
A merchant I became;
I earned a decent living there
And a respected name.

'But then one day while on a trip
To Epidamnum town,
My wife gave birth to two fine boys
Just as the sun went down.

'But in the golden evening light,'
Distraught Egeon sighed,
'On looking at my newborn sons
I suddenly espied...

'That they were like each other
To infinite degrees;
So much, in truth, it's fair to say
They looked just like two peas.

'You couldn't tell the boys apart —
One infant from his brother,
They lay there sleeping in their cribs
And each looked like the other.

'But then the most amazing thing
Of which you've ever heard:
Within an hour of their birth
Right there and then occurred...

'The birth of two more lovely boys.
I swear to you by God,
That these two infants also looked
Like two peas in a pod.

'Their mother and her husband
Were poor as poor could be,
And so I said, "I pray, good sir,
Give your two boys to me.

' "They can become the servants
To my two children here;
I'll see your boys are cared for well,
I pray be of good cheer,

' "For here is money that will help
The pair of you get through."
And so the deal was done right there –
It seemed the thing to do.

'They took the money gratefully,
So glad they'd found a way
To find the lads a decent home
And also make it pay.

'The boys became a valued part
Of our family,
Very close to our two sons
And to my wife and me.

'And so our life went on until
My wife spoke out one day:
"I'm tired of Epidamnum.
Can we go home, I pray?"

'I didn't really want to go
But said we'd make the trip,
So we set sail for Syracuse
Next day, aboard a ship.

'But shortly after leaving
Black clouds began to form,
And we were caught within an hour
In an almighty storm.

'The sailors all saw straightaway
The ship could not survive;
But they had just one strategy
To keep them all alive...

'And that was to escape the ship
They knew would surely sink –
So that is what the cowards did,
Right then, and in a wink.

'They launched small boats and all climbed in,
But left me there on board
With my dear wife and all four boys –
That is the truth, my lord.'

The duke was nodding gravely.
'What happened then?' he said.
'How in the world did you escape?
By rights you should be dead.'

'You speak the truth, my gracious lord,
But when the going's rough
It heightens your resolve and, well,
I guess it makes you tough.

'I tied my sons right there and then
Onto a broken mast;
Likewise the two, young servant boys,
And told them to hold fast.

'And then I bade my desperate wife
To hold the mast like me,
And with much trepidation,
We jumped into the sea.

'We watched the stricken ship drive on
And break up on a rock,
And once within that raging storm
Our mast was thrown amok.

'And then with an almighty noise
The great mast broke in two;
Wife, eldest boy and servant
All disappeared from view.

'The frightened younger lads and I,
Upon that ocean vast,
Just hung on tightly for our lives
To our small piece of mast.

'Like matchsticks we were thrown around
All through the rain-lashed night,
But then I glimpsed my poor dear wife –
'Twas just a glancing sight.

'A fishing boat was saving them;
I thanked the heavens' Lord,
For I believed they were quite safe
As they were pulled aboard.

'And then a mighty, crashing wave
Carried the boys and me
Away into the storm filled night,
Across the inky sea.

'I fought against the angry waves,
Did everything I could
To save those boys there in my charge –
I clung on to the wood.

'And then – as with my wife before,
A fishing boat appeared,
And happily, they snatched us from
The death which I had feared.

'They took us back to Syracuse,
Through raging seas – so wild,
And since that day I've never heard
Of wife or eldest child.

'My younger son grew curious,
When later he was told
Of what had happened on that night;
At eighteen he was bold.

'He said, "I'll go and search for them,
They must be somewhere, dad."
Now how could I refuse his wish?
He's a persuasive lad.

'And so I finally agreed
To what he wished to do,
Yet with a quaking in my heart
That I might lose him too.

'But then I hoped he'd find my wife,
And end my wretched tears;
I thought that he might find her though
She had been lost for years.

'So off he went and took with him
His loyal serving lad;
I freely do admit to you
Their going made me sad.

'And then on hearing nothing,
Worries set off anew,
For it is seven years ago
Since my boy said "Adieu".

'And for the last five of these years
I've had but little peace,
For I have searched for him and been
As far afield as Greece.

'And finally I landed here,
For though it meant great danger
I hoped that I might be ignored
Because I was a stranger.

'I knew I risked great peril
By ever coming here,
But hoping I would find my son
I overcame my fear.

'And now the worst has happened
And I shall lose my life,
But I would die a happy man
If I could see my wife.'

The duke was moved by all of this –
By all he heard and saw.
He said, 'I'd spare you if I could
But I can't change the law.

'But you shall have a further day
To beg or cadge or plead,
To somehow get your hands upon
The thousand marks you need.'

Egeon though just looked askance –
Despair across his face;
Whatever was the point of this
Unlooked for day of grace?

He knew no-one in Ephesus;
It just delayed his end,
For in that place he dare not hope
To find a single friend.

But hold a moment, for right there
In that unfriendly town,
Were people who could soon dispel
Sad, old Egeon's frown.

For at that time in Ephesus
There dwelt the very ones
For whom he sought so fervently –
Yes, his beloved sons.

The older son had lived right there
For twenty years or more;
The younger had arrived that day,
Despite the town's cruel law.

These lads had both the selfsame name.
Confusing? – Yes, I know.
Both were called Antipholus.
A nuisance – yes, and so...

To tell them both apart we must
Apply this simple ruse:
The younger twin, Antipholus,
Will be of Syracuse.

And to the older of the pair,
We now assign the name,
Antipholus of Ephesus –
Named hence from whence he came;

For he had lived in Ephesus
For many long years thus,
It is the ideal name by which
He should be known to us.

But it gets more confusing still
As both lads had close by –
The servants whom their dad had bought;
Now this will make you sigh...

For *they* both have the selfsame name,
And still look like each other:
Dromio – each one is called
The same as his twin brother.

Thus one of them is Dromio
Of Ephesus, and so
The other is 'of Syracuse' –
And now this fact you know...

To make the story easier,
So you can understand,
We shall devise a little ruse
To lend a helping hand.

Antipholus of Syracuse
Becomes Antipholus S,
We'll give his man an S as well,
And this should ease the mess.

And thus of course, Antipholus
Of Ephesus will be
Along with servant Dromio,
Attended by an E.

So back now to our story.
As I've already told,
Antipholus E had lived right there –
And he was rich and bold.

For he had been befriended by
The duke, some years before;
He'd been a soldier and had then
Shown bravery in war.

And so the duke, as just reward,
('For all you've done,' he'd said),
Betrothed him to a lovely lass
And so the pair had wed.

This lady, Adriana,
Was rich and also fair,
And they were living in the town
When Egeon came there.

Also with Antipholus E
Was someone else we know:
His faithful servant and good friend –
The young lad, Dromio.

Then in another part of town,
We find the second twin.
Antipholus S had just arrived –
So close to all his kin.

That he had come from Syracuse
Meant he should watch his back;
A friend there lets him know just how
He can avoid all flak.

'Say you're from Epidamnum,'
The crafty pal had said.
'For if you don't, you may well find
You quickly end up dead.

'An old man out of Syracuse
Was caught sometime today,
And he's about to lose his life
Because he cannot pay...

'The thousand marks the duke requires –
It's really very sad.'
Antipholus S had no idea
The friend spoke of his dad.

Antipholus then quickly sent
Young Dromio S to find
An inn where they could spend the night –
Where they could both unwind.

Whilst Dromio S went looking,
Antipholus walked some more,
But glancing up he was surprised
At what he thought he saw.

For Dromio S was coming back –
Already – in a tick;
Surely he'd not booked the inn...
How had he been so quick?

But this was Dromio E, to whom
Antipholus S then said,
'Why are you back so quickly?'
Dromio shook his head.

He said, 'My mistress bids you come
To dinner right away.'
'What mistress?' asked Antipholus.
'Who is this lady, pray?'

'Why, your dear wife,' the lad replied.
Antipholus lost his cool.
'I do not have a wife,' he said.
'Why do you play the fool?'

Dromio E thought this just fun
And told him once again
That dinner was awaiting him;
He made his plea in vain.

Antipholus S then beat him
And said, 'Upon my life,
You are a cheeky servant boy
For I don't have a wife.'

Dromio E then ran off home.
When Adriana heard
Her husband had denied her thus –
Of all that had occurred...

She fell into a jealous rage.
Her spouse had ceased to care.
What in the world was going on?
'He's having an affair!'

She found out where her 'husband' was,
Where he had last been seen,
And off she went with all due haste –
Prepared to vent her spleen.

And on arriving there she found
Antipholus S, of course;
She thought the showdown that would come
Might lead to a divorce.

For she was quite determined
That she would gain the truth,
So when she found him there, she yelled;
The poor man just cried, 'Strewth!'

He didn't have an inkling
Who this strange lass could be.
She cried, 'You've got another love.
You've been untrue to me.'

He said he didn't know her
But she replied to this,
'You are my husband, my true love.'
And tried to plant a kiss.

At last she said, 'Come home at once,
My husband – I insist.'
Antipholus S could see no way
To anymore resist.

He went then to his brother's house
And there sat down to dine
With his dear 'wife' – her sister too:
They had fine food and wine.

Dromio S had come as well
And found his way into
The kitchen, where the female cook
Just stuck to him like glue.

She said she was his own dear wife –
So more confusion here;
But even greater trouble now
Was swiftly drawing near.

Antipholus E approached the house,
Returning home to eat,
But when he knocks upon the door
His servants there entreat…

'Be gone at once, good sir, because
Our mistress has made clear
She's dining with her husband now.'
He cried, 'What's that I hear?'

He roared and remonstrated,
He yelled and yelled some more,
But these obedient servants
Would not come to the door.

Finally he went away,
A most unhappy soul;
To find out what was going on
Had now become his goal.

~ ~ ~

Antipholus S, a puzzled man
Is finishing his meal;
He's sick of Adriana
And all her crazy spiel,

So he is keen to get away;
He puts down fork and knife,
Preparing his excuses now
To leave this cranky 'wife'.

He doesn't like her very much,
But her sister – who's there too –
Well she's a different matter;
He takes a different view.

The truth is that he fancies her
But that will have to wait,
Though he's determined at some time
He'll try to get a date.

Luciana was the sister –
But, despite her being there,
He apologised for leaving
And got up from his chair.

'I really must be on my way,
So thank you for the food;
I have appointments I must keep –
I don't mean to be rude.'

And with these lame excuses
He got onto his feet
And finding servant Dromio
They made a quick retreat.

The pair of them just shook their heads,
And each one wore a frown,
But they were pleased to be back in
The bustle of the town.

But more confusion was in store;
They were about to meet
A goldsmith, who came up to them
As they walked down the street.

'Here's your golden chain,' he said.
'Made specially for you.'
At this Antipholus S replied –
Unsure of what to do…

'There is some error here, I fear,
I'm not the one you seek.'
The goldsmith testily replied,
'You ordered it last week.'

He forced the chain upon the lad
And then he went away.
Antipholus S then said, 'Let's go
And board a ship today.'

He spoke to his man Dromio,
'I do not like it here.
The people all seem crazy –
They're off their heads, I fear.'

Meanwhile the poor old goldsmith
Was in trouble down the road,
For officers were having words
About some cash he owed.

These chaps were in the process
Of arresting him, but then
Antipholus E came into view;
The goldsmith said, 'Wait men.

'This man will pay my debt for me,
For I gave him a chain
And if you let me speak to him,
I know that he'll explain...

'That it can all be sorted out.
He'll pay the cash I owe.'
Antipholus E, when he was asked,
Just didn't want to know.

He said, 'I never had the chain.'
And thus began a row.
The goldsmith remonstrated,
'You had the chain just now.

'You put it in your pocket.'
Antipholus E said, 'No!'
The officers at last declared
That they would have to throw...

The goldsmith into jail until
His debts were duly paid.
The goldsmith then, with angry words,
Endeavoured to persuade...

The officers to take in charge
Antipholus E as well.
'He owes me for the chain,' he said,
'So he should share my cell.'

The officers had had enough;
This all must be curtailed,
So they arrested both of them
And took them to be jailed.

But as Antipholus E was dragged
To prison, he then saw
Young Dromio S – his brother's man –
So he told him the score...

And ordered him to go at once
And tell his wife to send
Some money – but poor Dromio S
Just didn't comprehend.

Then thinking that his master
Desired him to return
To Adriana's house, he went –
For he did not discern...

This wasn't *his* Antipholus.
So off he duly went,
Although he really didn't know
What all this nonsense meant.

Well, Adriana gave him cash,
But as he thus returned,
He saw Antipholus (that's S)
Who with confusion burned;

For everywhere he went he found
The folk all called him 'friend'.
The kindness people showed to him,
He couldn't comprehend.

And then when Dromio S came up
And said, 'My master pray,
How did you slip the officer?
How did you get away?'

And then went on to add, 'Look here,
I've got this cash for you,'
Antipholus S was forced to think
His servant was mad too.

He'd really lost his mind for sure;
Antipholus was astounded:
All these crazy goings-on
Had left him quite dumbfounded.

And then to cap the whole thing off
A lady now came up,
Who claimed that this Antipholus
Had been to her to sup.

And then she asked him for a chain
He'd promised as a gift.
He said, 'What are you speaking of?'
And then gave her short shrift.

But she continued to insist.
He said she was a fool,
And when she carried on again
He really lost his cool.

He said she was a sorceress.
She countered, 'Where's my ring?'
He answered, 'I have no idea,
For I don't know a thing...

'About a ring or who you are.'
And then he ran away.
He wouldn't hear another word
Of what she had to say.

An explanation to all this
Would be in order here.
I must ensure that everything
Makes sense and is quite clear.

When Antipholus E was sent
Packing from his door,
He thought his wife was in a mood –
He was convinced for sure...

That it was just a jealous rant
From his bad-tempered wife.
He thought, 'I'll get revenge on her,
I swear it on my life.'

So he'd gone to this lady
And promised her a chain.
He did it just because his wife
Had once more caused him pain.

The chain was one he'd ordered –
Supposedly a gift –
For his own wife, to make amends
For yet another rift.

But in his fit of pique, he'd thought
He'd give the chain away
To this good lady, though he guessed
There'd be a price to pay.

He didn't have it on him
But said that he would bring
The chain a little later on,
So she gave him her ring.

It was done in but a moment,
Impulsive – some would say;
But with no further thought at all,
She gave the ring away;

For she was happy that she'd have
The chain – a lovely thing –
And in a passion had then said,
'Here take my favourite ring.'

So when she had confronted
Antipholus S, she thought
It was his brother, who to her
Had sadly fallen short.

For he denied all knowledge of
The gift he'd promised her:
He really must be mad she thought,
Or just a rotten cur.

At last she had decided
He wasn't only bad;
No, there could be no doubt at all –
He'd gone completely mad.

She went to Adriana,
And said, 'It's sad to say,
Your husband has gone crazy –
It happened just today.'

Adriana did not doubt
These words for she knew how
He'd been so strange at dinner
And how – with furrowed brow...

He'd said he wasn't married,
That she was not his wife;
That he'd not been to Ephesus
Before in all his life.

So now convinced, she went to him,
Imprisoned in the jail,
And paid the money out again,
So he was granted bail.

She had her servants tie him up
With ropes, and had him thrown
Into a dim and darkened room
And left him there alone.

Dromio E was locked up too –
They told the selfsame tale –
And though they were locked up at home
It seemed just like a jail.

But then a little later on
Somebody came to tell
That Adriana's husband walked
In town and looked quite well.

And Dromio was with him –
They must have broken loose!
How could this thing have happened?
How did they slip the noose?

When Adriana heard of this
She ran to fetch him home,
Determined she would tie him down
So that he couldn't roam.

She found him by a convent –
That's who she *thought* she saw;
It was, of course, her yet unknown
Bewildered brother-in-law.

Antipholus S was standing there
With Dromio S as well.
The goldsmith there was giving
Antipholus sheer hell.

They'd let the goldsmith out of jail,
And now he cried, 'By heck,
Why did you so deny you had
That chain around your neck?'

Antipholus S was saying,
'You freely gave this chain,
And since that hour I've never clapped
My eyes on you again.'

Adriana then appeared
Right before them then,
And she had brought along with her
A bunch of burley men.

They tried to grab Antipholus,
His servant Dromio too;
They ran into the convent,
The smartest thing to do.

They begged for shelter in the shrine;
The abbess then came out
To ascertain what all the fuss
Outside had been about.

She was a wise old lady,
Said she was not prepared
To give the two men up just yet –
Who both seemed very scared...

Until she heard the details
Of what they were accused.
Adriana was annoyed –
Oh, she was not amused.

She said her faithless husband had
Completely lost his mind.
'It really is his fault that he
Is in this awful bind.'

The abbess sighed, 'You should have nagged
If he has been untrue.
You should have told him all the time
It's not the thing to do.'

'I did! I did!' the wife replied.
'I told him all the time.
I said that doing what he did
Was tantamount to crime.

'I told him off when in our bed,
And when he tried to eat.
I told him off throughout the meal,
Until he left his seat.

'And when alone, I told him,'
Then Adriana said
What a rotten man he was –
The worthless life he led.

'And when we were in company
I still would have a go –
Oh yes, sweet abbess, in all truth
I really let him know.'

The abbess had found out for sure
What drove the poor man mad.
She said, 'I think you've acted in
A way that's very bad.

'These actions you've recounted,
Done time and time again,
Would drive a really noble man
Around the bend – insane!

'A jealous woman is, for sure,
Much worse, I say, forsooth,
Than deadly poison deep within
A mad dog's fearsome tooth.'

The sister, Luciana, said,
'Why take this lying down?'
But Adriana thus replied
With an embarrassed frown...

'The abbess speaks the truth – I see
The error of my ways,
For I have acted woefully
On very many days.'

But still she said, 'My husband,
Who's cowering in there
Should now be handed over
Into my loving care.'

The abbess wouldn't give him up;
She really was a gem.
She said, 'I will take care of him.'
Then closed her gates on them.

~ ~ ~

As all this had been happening,
We sadly have to say,
Egeon's single day of grace
Had quickly slipped away.

And he would die at sunset,
They'd execute him there:
Close to the convent, he'd been told
He'd make his final prayer.

But at that very moment
Some people came along:
The duke was with Egeon,
Accompanied by a throng.

When Adriana saw the duke
She stopped him in his track.
'The abbess has my husband
And will not give him back.'

But as she spoke, who should appear,
Quite sane and looking spruce –
Her husband and his Dromio;
The pair had just got loose.

He complained, as well he might;
He told the duke his tale,
How his bad wife had called him mad;
Oh, how he did regale...

The duke with all the awful things
He said that he'd been through;
How he'd been locked up with his man –
Of how they broke out too.

And as he spoke, his wife stood by,
Surprise upon her face.
Was this her husband standing here
Or just one more nutcase?

For she believed her husband
Was in the convent there;
She shook her head and wrung her hands
In her perplexed despair.

Egeon looked upon his son
And thought he was none other
Than the boy who'd left his home
To find his mum and brother.

But this of course was not the case;
It was Antipholus E
To whom he spoke and who replied,
'You are not known to me.'

Egeon was astonished
To be denied this way:
When he said, 'We have not met.'
What could Egeon say?

He thought his son was just borne down
By some strange silly whim;
That some weird illness was the cause
Of his not knowing him.

But as he spoke, the convent door
Was opened – there appeared
The abbess with the two young men;
Now this was really weird.

Everyone there present, gasped.
Could all of this be true?
And Adriana saw she had
Not one spouse there, but two!

There stood Antipholus himself
And Dromio S as well.
The duke recalled Egeon's tale,
When he had heard him tell…

The details of the shipwreck –
So said, 'It seems to me
The sons of this poor man right here
Are who these lads must be.'

Oh what a joyful moment
As Egeon hugged his sons;
A reunion as memorable
As history's greatest ones.

But then the lady abbess
Completed all their joys.
She said, 'I am Egeon's wife
And these are my two boys.'

Explaining that the fisherman
Who'd rescued them – all three –
Had sold the boys, when they arrived
Safely in port from sea.

And so she'd joined the convent
To ease her desperate grief,
And here she'd found some solace –
And sanctified relief.

In time, by holy conduct,
Avoiding selfish ploys,
She'd been elected abbess,
And thus had found her boys.

Amid these joyful happenings
One thing they all forgot
Was that poor old Egeon
Was still in quite a spot.

He was still under sentence,
And could quite soon be dead.
Antipholus E spoke out at once:
'I'll pay the fee,' he said.

The duke though would have none of it.
'He's pardoned,' he then cried.
'He is excused the thousand marks –
Proclaim it far and wide.

'And he shall be a free man
Within our country here,
And from this moment on he is
Completely in the clear.'

They walked into the convent,
A most contented band.
Everyone was happy that
The fates had played this hand...

And brought them all together –
A family again –
And so this doesn't leave too much
For us to now explain.

The Dromios, of course, were pleased,
Each one to meet his twin;
The pair of them just walked around
With a perpetual grin.

And both said that they'd never seen,
In life or picture books,
A person like their brother there
Who had such handsome looks.

And Adriana, for her part,
Showed jealousy no more;
She listened to the council of
Her gracious mother-in-law.

Antipholus S, as we well know
Had had a roving eye;
Since seeing Luciana,
Well, all he'd done was sigh.

So he proposed she marry him,
And, quickly she said, 'Yes!'
And thus their marriage marked the end
Of all this silly mess.

Egeon lived on happily
For many fruitful years,
Surrounded by his family,
With no more grief or tears.

No more wandering the world
With all its many terrors,
And no more time confused within
A comedy of errors.

*'I want Antonio's pound of flesh,
I'll have my bond,' said he*

THE MERCHANT OF VENICE

Antonio – a merchant,
Lived in Venice town of old.
He was a wheeler-dealer;
A guy who bought and sold.

He was known both far and wide
For kindness without end,
Because he'd shell out hard earned cash
To help a needy friend.

He wouldn't ask for interest,
He wouldn't charge a fee.
He'd hand the money over,
They'd get the loan for free.

These gestures went down very well
With everyone he knew,
Except tight-fisted Shylock,
A moneylender too.

Shylock objected strongly
Through all his ancient bones,
Because he made great profit
Charging interest on loans.

Antonio thought that he was mean
And – fond of playing games –
When he bumped into Shylock,
He'd often call him names.

Shylock bore this with patience
And let him have his say,
But then beneath his breath he vowed,
'I'll be avenged some day.'

~ ~ ~

Bassanio – a nobleman –
Was Antonio's best friend,
But though he was of noble blood,
Had little cash to spend.

He'd spend whatever cash he had
As men of rank will do,
And when his funds ran really short
Antonio helped him through.

One day Bassanio exclaimed,
'Antonio, I'm bewitched
By this really gorgeous girl.
I'm hoping to get hitched.'

He said, 'I love her dearly,
She really is a honey;
What makes it even better,
She's got pots and pots of money.

'If she'll become my loving bride
'Twill mean I'm not so broke.
With money and a wife I'll solve
Two problems at a stroke.

'But I need cash to aid my bid,'
He then went on to say.
'I need three thousand ducats and
I need them right away.

'The money is important
So that, my friend, I can,
Equip myself and suitably,
To be a worthy man.'

Antonio was very quick
And eager now to say,
That he would help Bassanio
In this financial way.

But at the time – he had to state –
He had no cash in hand,
But said he'd ask old Shylock
To lend him the three grand.

He wasn't really worried
As he had ships at sea,
Due back in Venice by next month
With spices, gold and tea.

His standing in old Venice town
Of course, was widely known,
And once the ships returned he'd have
The funds to clear the loan.

~ ~ ~

So they went to visit Shylock
To ask him for the loan.
A man who felt that disrespect
Was all he'd e'er been shown.

He stroked his beard and rolled his eyes
And fingered his lapel,
And then he said with thoughtfulness,
'Three thousand ducats – well.'

He stood for several moments –
Made not the slightest sound,
And then he asked, 'Antonio,
Shall by an oath be bound?'

They both confirmed that it was so.
'Three thousand ducats for
A period of just three months –
We do not ask for more.'

Shylock pondered long and hard.
His thoughts were base and low.
He thought about the merchant,
The good Antonio.

'I hate him for his fawning ways
And giving loans for free.
I suffer every day and from
His generosity.

'He gives out loans for nothing
And brings the rates right down.
It's hard to make a living now
Just anywhere in town.

'He hates me earning interest
Though I keep margins slim.
I will be cursed, there is no doubt
If I give help to him.

'But maybe I can see a way,
If I am any judge,
To catch him out quite unawares
And feed my ancient grudge.'

Antonio lost patience.
'Shylock, d'you hear?' says he.
'Answer me right now and say
You'll lend the cash to me.'

Shylock thought before responding
In a quiet, angry way.
'You want my cash, yet did you not
Spit at me yesterday?

'You call me dog but has a dog
Got any cash to spend?
Is it really possible
He'd have three grand to lend?

'And you expect me also
To let your insults go.'
Antonio said, 'Then lend it
As if it's to a foe.

'For I am like to do again
Those things I've done before.
I'll spurn you and it's likely that
I'll spit on you once more.

'So treat me as an enemy
And then I'm sure you'll see
You'll gain more pleasure if you can
Exact a penalty!'

'Oh how you storm!' old Shylock cried.
'Won't you be friends with me?
To prove my generosity,
Why, have the loan for free.'

Antonio was astounded.
The offer was most kind.
It was without a trace of doubt
The best deal he would find.

Bassanio said, 'What kindness.'
But Shylock spoke again,
And though his words were devious
He spoke in merry vein.

'Come with me and seal a bond
And let us also say,
That if the bond is not repaid
By the allotted day...

'Why then,' he said beginning
To weave a devilish mesh,
'Let us agree you'll forfeit
A pound of your own flesh.

'This to be cut and taken,'
Lightly then says he,
'Antonio – from your body
Wherever pleases me.'

Antonio cried, 'I will agree.
I'll gladly sign the bond.'
Bassanio said he was convinced
Antonio had been conned.

He said it was a bad deal
Antonio had just bought,
But Shylock smiled and murmured that
The deal was 'merely sport'.

Antonio signed the bond and said,
'My ships will soon arrive.
Old Shylock will not get my flesh.
You'll see – I will survive.'

~ ~ ~

The girl Bassanio loved and was
Now set to woo and win,
Lived with her trusted servants –
She'd lost her closest kin.

She owned vast lands and stately home.
She was a wealthy dame.
And Portia of Belmont
Was this good lady's name.

She was a pretty maiden.
Very nice – and clever too.
Suitors came from far and wide
And sometimes had to queue.

Her father knew a lot of men
Would want her for their bride,
So he'd devised a clever plan
Some months before he died.

A most ingenious scheme it was –
He'd had a wily touch –
A way to find a worthy groom
For the child he loved so much.

His plan was like a lottery,
Three riddles to be read,
Each carved upon a casket made
Of silver, gold or lead.

The suitors had to make a choice
And if they found inside,
A picture of fair Portia,
They'd win her for their bride.

But if they were unfortunate
And chose a casket there,
Containing something else, well then –
Although it seems unfair...

They were required to swear an oath
That never in their life,
Would they seek out another
To take then as their wife.

And they must leave Belmont estate
Although it pained them so;
Leave Portia there – and waiting for
A winning beau to show.

Many suitors tried their luck
But failed and went away.
Sweet Portia was delighted but
Of course she didn't say.

Her thoughts were of Bassanio
Whom she had met before,
And so her heart beat very fast
When he knocked at her door.

He went straight to the casket room,
Wild thoughts raced through his head,
But concentrating hard he chose
The one made out of lead.

It was the very hardest choice
He'd made in all his life,
But it became the one to win
Dear Portia for his wife.

For in that leaden casket
He happily found there
An image – oh so wonderful,
Of Portia sweet and fair.

And with it lay a parchment scroll
Which said he'd chosen true,
And said, 'The lady Portia's hand,
Now sir, belongs to you.'

And then the scroll went on to say,
'If you are pleased with this,
Why turn unto your lady now
And claim her with a kiss.'

And so Bassanio kissed her
And to *his* lady said,
'I really can't believe that now
The two of us can wed.'

And then he quietly confessed
He'd been a two faced lad,
For noble birth and ancestry
Were really all he had.

But Portia was most gracious
And said she didn't mind,
For though he had no money
She thought him quite a find.

She said that all she had was his
And then one special thing,
She handed him affectionately –
A lovely, jewelled ring.

Bassanio gave grateful thanks,
A grave look on his brow.
He put it on his finger
And made this solemn vow.

'I'll wear this ring forever,
Not let it from my sight.
'Twill stay upon my finger
Each morning, noon and night.

'And if this ring is parted
At any time,' he said,
'From here upon my finger –
Then know Bassanio's dead.'

~ ~ ~

They began their plans to wed.
There seemed no time to lose,
But then a messenger arrived
And he brought fearful news.

He had hastened from Antonio.
The news was bad indeed.
Bassanio turned ghostly white
As they all watched him read.

His hands began to tremble,
His countenance looked bleak.
'What steals the colour,' Portia asked,
'From good Bassanio's cheek?'

'Sweet Portia, gentle lady,'
Bassanio softly said,
'These sad and dreadful words are quite
The worst I've ever read.

'For when I first professed my love
I said I had no wealth,
That all I had was my good name
And my abundant health.

'But I should have truly told you
My funds were really small.
In fact I should have made it plain,
I have no funds at all.

'And even less than nothing.
My state is really bad,
For I'm in debt and must confess
To acting like a cad.

'Antonio lent me money
To win you for my wife,
And now it seems this favour
Will cost my friend his life.'

And then he read Antonio's note.
'Bassanio,' it said,
'All my ships are lost at sea
Which means I'll soon be dead.

'I owe my bond to Shylock.
It's what I now must give,
And when he's had his pound of flesh
How can I hope to live?'

And then he asked Bassanio
To visit ere he died.
'Oh go at once and take some gold,'
Fraught Portia quickly cried.

'Let Shylock have ten times his bond
To save your dear friend's head,
But first of all I must insist
The two of us be wed.

'For then my money will be yours,
I'll be your legal wife,
And then you can depart with haste
To save Antonio's life.'

~ ~ ~

Once wed Bassanio hurried off,
He went to save his friend,
But when he got to Venice found
Old Shylock wouldn't bend.

The date the loan was due had passed:
In fact by quite a while.
And Shylock claimed his bond outright,
Insisting on a trial.

He craved his pound of flesh in full
And he was heard to say,
'I'll have my bond, it is my due
And I *will* have my way.'

And so a day had now been fixed,
This strange case would be heard
Before the Duke of Venice who
Would have the final word.

~ ~ ~

When Bassanio left for Venice
His wife encouraged him,
But Portia thought that Shylock's threat
Was not an idle whim.

She feared the worst would happen.
Shylock would win the day.
She wondered how she could assist
And then worked out a way.

She had a distant cousin,
A lawyer by his trade;
She thought, 'He'll save Antonio
From Shylock's vicious blade.'

And sure he enough, he sent her robes
And notes how to proceed,
That she might plead the case in court
And get Antonio freed.

Portia and her maid got dressed
In robes they had been lent,
And then set off for Venice town
Armed with the notes he'd sent.

On arrival she was keen
To see the duke, to know,
If she could be the counsel for
Accused Antonio.

The duke declared that she could plead
Antonio's case in court.
He didn't rate her chances much,
But didn't voice this thought.

~ ~ ~

And so Antonio's trial began.
Portia's disguise was good,
So no-one recognised her in
Her lawyer's cape and hood.

'Shylock,' she said, 'the law is clear
There is no controversy,
Your bond is yours by right to have,
But can you not show mercy?'

Portia spoke of mercy,
How it was doubly blessed,
To those who gave and when received,
But as all present guessed...

Shylock would not change his mind.
He claimed his bond in full,
Insisting on his pound of flesh –
Her fine words had no pull.

Bassanio then offered
The three grand – even more –
But Shylock simply shook his head
And cried, 'Apply the law!'

Portia said the law must stand
As laid down in the books.
'Oh wise young judge,' old Shylock cried,
'You're older than your looks.'

Portia asked to see the bond;
Perusing it she said,
'Shylock's due his pound of flesh
From everything I've read.'

She turned to Shylock pleading,
'Show mercy – take the cash.'
Shylock's answer flew right back,
Resolute, in a flash.

'I want Antonio's pound of flesh.
I'll have my bond,' said he.
'By my soul I promise you
Fine words can't alter me.'

Portia said, 'He has the right
To make this awful claim,
But Shylock take three times your bond –
Let mercy be your aim.'

Shylock cried, 'You seem to be
A worthy, upright judge,
And so I stand right by my bond
And vow I will not budge.

'Proceed to judgement – do it now
As noble judge you can.
Discharge with speed our Venice law,
Oh, excellent young man.'

Everyone in court now feared
For poor Antonio's life,
Portia told him to prepare
And Shylock whet his knife.

Shylock brandished his sharpened blade
In a vicious kind of way;
Portia asked Antonio,
'Have you last words to say?'

Antonio was very calm
Though close to his last breath.
He said that he'd prepared his mind
To meet untimely death.

He held Bassanio by the hand
And said, 'Don't grieve for me.
Commend me to your dear, sweet wife
Who I shan't live to see.'

Shylock cried, 'We're wasting time.
Give sentence right away.
I want to have my forfeit and
I'll brook no more delay.'

'It shall be so,' Portia replied.
'The forfeit must be paid.
Someone bring a set of scales
To see the flesh is weighed.

'And Shylock, you are now allowed
A pound of flesh – it's yours.
The court awards it to you
As does our city's laws.'

'Most rightful judge,' old Shylock cried.
'A sentence! Come prepare.'
He turned to face Antonio
With dark and evil stare.

His manner was triumphant;
He looked around the court;
It was clear he saw at last
The wicked end he sought.

'Oh upright judge!' he cried again,
'You're truly very fair.'
He raised his knife and cruelly told
His victim to 'Lay bare.'

'But stay your hand,' said Portia.
'One word must now be said;
Take care that when you cut the flesh
No drop of blood be shed.

'And Shylock when you take it,
Take no more than your due.
Just one pound is all the flesh
The law decrees to you'

Shylock stopped dead in his tracks,
Let out an anguished cry,
For he had hoped most fervently
Antonio would die.

'Is that the law?' he cried out loud.
Said Portia, 'It's a fact,
And if you doubt it Shylock –
Why come and check the Act.'

Shylock spat, 'I'll take the money.'
But she'd have none of it.
She told him he must take the flesh –
Take every little bit.

But then she warned, 'Take any blood
Or more than that laid down,
And by the law you then shall die.'
Well this made Shylock frown.

'Give me the cash!' he shouted out.
'And then just let me go.'
'Now tarry Shylock,' Portia said,
'There's more you need to know.

'You threatened good Antonio
To satisfy your hate,
And therefore half your worldly goods
Are forfeit to the state.

'Antonio has the other half.
It's what the law decrees,
And there's no point now Shylock
In any further pleas.

'But there is just one other thing,
Your life is forfeit too,
You can but pray the gracious duke
Sees fit to pardon you.'

The duke did spare old Shylock's life
Despite the havoc wrought –
And told him he was free to go:
He hurried from the court.

Then everyone thanked Portia
And said, 'Don't rush away.'
But she replied most graciously,
She really couldn't stay.

'We must reward you,' they all said,
'For everything you've done.'
Portia refused but then she saw
How she could have some fun.

And turning to Bassanio
She said, 'Give me one thing –
By way of a small keepsake,
Hand me that lovely ring.'

Bassanio was in a fix
For had he not once said,
If parted from the ring assume
That he was surely dead.

What would he tell his loving wife?
He knew not what to do,
But said, 'This rings a trifle,
Not good enough for you.

'I will not shame myself to give
This bauble to you sir,
I'll find the finest ring there is
And this I will confer.'

He said, 'I cannot part with this,
A gift from my dear wife,
For I gave her a solemn vow
'Twould stay with me for life.'

Portia said, 'Why that excuse
Saves men from everything.
I'm sure your wife would say that I
Deserved to have the ring.

'But let it rest, I will not beg,
So farewell and take care.'
She left the room with head held high
And left him standing there.

Antonio then spoke and said,
'My Lord Bassanio,
Let him have the ring for this
Is what you surely owe.

'Your worthy wife will understand.
She'll see you had no choice,
And I for one will back you up
And add my willing voice.'

Bassanio was now convinced
It was the proper thing,
So sent a friend to hurry off
To give the 'judge' the ring.

~ ~ ~

Portia returned to Belmont
So pleased she'd solved the mess,
And on arriving back at home
She put on normal dress.

And so she there awaited for
The party to return,
And now anticipation
Within her breast did burn.

She knew she'd acted cleverly
When all was said and done,
But now determined that she'd have
A little bit of fun.

～ ～ ～

When the others got to Belmont
They were a merry band,
Their talk was of the lawyer
Who'd lent a helping hand.

Then it was mentioned suddenly
That Lord Bassanio
Had handed the young lawyer
A ring – oh yes – 'twas so.

Bassanio spoke to himself,
'This is a nasty twist,
It would be best if I just cut
My hand clean off my wrist.

'And then perhaps by using
Every ounce of wit,
I could insist I lost the ring
By thus defending it.'

But Portia now spoke out and said,
'What ring gave you, I pray?
Not that, I hope, which I gave you
Upon our wedding day.'

Bassanio then softly said,
His face all pale and wan,
'My finger does not bear the ring.
I can't deny it's gone.

'But if you knew to whom I gave
My precious wedding ring,
And if you knew for whom I gave
The treasured, lovely ring.

'And if you could conceive for what
I gave away the ring,
And how unwillingly my dear
I left behind the ring...

'When nothing was acceptable
But that valued ring,
Well then your great displeasure
Would lose its righteous ring.'

Portia quickly came right back,
Her words were full of force,
Even though 'twas all a joke
She stayed true to her course.

'If you my lord had known the truth –
The virtue of the ring,
And half the worthiness of she
Who handed you the ring:

'Or held your honour sacrosanct
To safely guard the ring,
Why then my lord you would have not
Thus parted with the ring.'

Then Portia smiled and sweetly said,
'Take this new one then, I pray.'
Bassanio saw the ring she held
Was the one he gave away.

Said Portia, 'I'm the lawyer
Who saved Antonio's life.'
Bassanio in amazement hugged
His wise, resourceful wife.

He said, 'Were you the lawyer?
Oh such a devious plot.
To think I saw you there in court
And strangely knew you not.'

And then he said, 'Forgive me please,
And now I vow one thing,
Never again will I lose sight
Of this, my wedding ring.'

Then Portia laughed and kissed him
And to Antonio said,
'There's tremendous news within
This letter I've just read.

'Your ships have come back safely,
They're docked at Venice quay.'
Antonio raised his arms and said,
'What wonderful news for me.'

They laughed and were so thankful
Things had turned out this way.
Then Portia said, 'It's time to rest
For it is nearly day.'

*'For I would have some words with you
About my new decree'*

LOVE'S LABOUR'S LOST

King Ferdinand of great Navarre
Bade three lords, 'Come to me,
For I would have some words with you
About my new decree.'

And so Berowne and Longaville,
And also Lord Dumaine,
Asked him, 'What do you wish of us?
Please make your meaning plain.'

The king replied, 'I would impose
Upon you three lords here,
A duty that will do you good
For many a long year.

'For I intend to make Navarre
A centre of great learning,
And wish for knowledge – that alone –
To fill your every yearning.

'So now, my lords, I ask you all
To join me in my quest;
And please don't look at me that way
As this is not a jest.

'For we will spend the next three years
In study and we'll keep
A strict regime of fasting and
Restrict our hours of sleep.

'And most of all, we will suspend
All fraternising stuff
With ladies, and although you'll find
That this will be quite tough...

'It's crucial to this plan of mine
That women are denied.'
Two of the lords there said, 'All right.'
But Lord Berowne just sighed,

Then quickly gathering his thoughts,
He said, 'Beloved king,
This all sounds most commendable
But you forget one thing.

'For in this contract here you say,
No woman can defile
Our firm resolve to live alone –
Or come within a mile.

'Your court will be for men alone,
And we three will be blamed
If we are found with women fair –
You say we will be shamed.

'Yet even as you ask this thing –
Exert your royal power;
As you implore it's for our good –
Right now, upon this hour...

'A princess from fair France arrives;
She's coming here today.
Surely the princess, once she's here
Blows all resolve away –

'For you should not converse with her.'
The king said, 'But she's here
Upon a diplomatic trip –
I must have words, I fear.'

Berowne then sighed and slowly said,
'Though I'm loathe to agree,
I'll sign and thus I do, my lord,
Accept this new decree.'

~ ~ ~

Lord Boyet's with the French princess –
He gives advice and aid,
For though she is of royal blood
She still is but a maid.

He tells her, 'Please remember that
You've come here in the main
To talk about the status of
The land of Aquitaine.'

The princess is accompanied
By three young ladies fair:
Rosaline and Katharine –
Maria too is there.

The ladies are all talking
About Navarre's great lords,
What dashing men they seem to be
With capes and ruffs and swords.

The men are all so bold and brave
And handsome and so kind.
Now could it be that these three girls
Have romance on their mind?

Maria once saw Longaville
In Normandy one day.
'I think he is a fine, young man,'
The girl was heard to say.

And so she told the other two,
'There is no man to match
Lord Longaville – I'm sure he'd be
A really worthy catch.'

Then Katharine said, 'I do believe
That Lord Dumaine is nice.
He's noble, honest – oh so fine –
Quite free of any vice.'

Rosaline on hearing this,
Said, 'I think best of all
Is Lord Berowne; he's so well built,
So muscular and tall.

'I spent an evening with him once –
He had me in a fit
With all his funny jokes and tales
And with his ready wit.'

And thus the young girls carried on
With these romantic tales
About their brief encounters with
These dashing, brave, young males.

But then the king himself comes in
And makes his way towards
The princess and her ladies there,
Attended by his lords.

He says, 'I'm very sorry but
You can't stay with us gents.
I hope you'll be quite comfortable
Within these lovely tents.'

The princess had been told about
The king's three year decree,
And though she didn't like the tent
She said, 'It's fine with me.'

She reads a letter from her dad
Who is the King of France,
And while she reads, King Ferdinand
Is in a love-filled trance.

She says, 'The Aquitaine belongs
To France.' and then she frowns.
The king replies, 'But what about
Our hundred thousand crowns?

'For that is what you owe to us,
And once the sum is paid,
Why you can have the Aquitaine
And we'll complete the trade.'

The princess says, 'You will receive
The proof we've paid quite soon;
In fact I think you should get word
Before tomorrow noon.'

But while all this was going on
It's no surprise to hear
The men had nobbled Lord Boyet,
To get the old chap's ear.

They asked him questions all at once
About the ladies there.
Dumaine said, 'Is there any chance
That Katharine might care?'

And Longaville said, 'I do think
Maria's quite sublime,
But tell me, sir, in honesty
If I do waste my time?'

Berowne then said of Rosaline,
'My lord, she is the best,
But am I doomed to failure
In this, my lovelorn quest?'

Then Lord Boyet listened to
The princess and the king
As they discussed their business
And clearly saw one thing...

As if it were in words of fire,
As if it had been written:
The king was quite entranced, enthralled –
In fact, completely smitten.

And when the king had left that day
Boyet – without ado,
Told the princess straight away,
'The king's in love with you.'

~ ~ ~

And so the four young gentlemen –
The nobles and their king –
Are deep in love, although they swore
They would not do this thing.

When each of them is safe away
Out of the other's sight,
Each one sits down with pen and ink
And they begin to write.

For they have all turned poet and
Compose their verses to
The lady who lights up their life;
To tell her, 'I love you'.

So they ignore their solemn vows:
What if the others find
That they have broken the decree,
Completely changed their mind?

Berowne, once finished, then commands
A servant, 'Take this note
To Rosaline, but make quite sure
It's tucked beneath your coat.'

He didn't want to take the chance
The others would find out.
They mustn't have an inkling
Of what he was about.

For truthfully, he was amazed
That love had struck him so –
That he was now resolved to be
Sweet Rosaline's own beau.

He mused awhile and spoke these words,
'Never in my life
Would I have thought that I would love –
That I would seek a wife.

'But now I love, I sigh, I groan,
But most of all I pray
That Rosaline will take me as
Her husband, one fine day.'

Then later on Berowne climbs up
One of the royal trees
And makes himself a hiding place;
Then, looking down, he sees...

The king below with poetry –
He's reading it out loud!
Its contents show he's thrown away
All that he has avowed.

The poem which the king declaims
Up to the heavens above,
Is all about the French princess
With whom he's now in love.

The king in turn hears Longaville
As he is reading too –
A sonnet to Maria;
It's lovelorn through and through.

Then Longaville pricks up his ears –
It will be no surprise
That he now hears Dumaine proclaim
His love has such blue eyes.

He was professing to the world
That Katharine, his love
Was quite the fairest in the land –
His own beloved dove.

And thus it was that these three youths,
Each secretly, had heard,
The other breaking his strict vow,
Every fervent word.

And so they then admit the truth,
Each one of them in turn.
The king says, 'We're in trouble if
Berowne should ever learn...

'That we've so quickly thrown away
Our firm resolve and vow.'
But as he spoke Berowne himself
Descended from his bough.

He says, 'You each have been untrue
And chosen to ignore
The solemn oath that we all took –
Denied the vow we swore.'

They looked around shamefacedly
And each of them came clean.
Berowne then really rubbed it in,
How sneaky they had been.

But then his servant comes and says,
'I got into a mix;
The wrong note I gave Rosaline.'
Berowne was in a fix!

For as he spoke he handed him
The poem and he said,
'So here it is, unopened sire.'
Berowne then turned bright red.

He grabbed the note and tore it up,
Then threw it on the ground.
Dumaine though picked the pieces up,
And then of course he found...

Berowne had also been untrue
And thrown aside his vow.
The king declared, 'We're all as one.
So what should we do now?'

Turning to Berowne he said,
'Well, you must find a way
To prove our loving's lawful,
To show that it's okay.'

Berowne was nimble on his feet,
He had an agile mind,
And it would surely help him out
If he could quickly find...

A way to justify the fact
That they had all denied
The oath they solemnly had sworn –
For each of them had lied.

He glanced around at his dear friends,
At their expectant looks,
And said, 'Love teaches many things
That can't be found in books.

'And so I think that when we love
We also study too,
So following our heart's desire
Is quite the thing to do.'

And then he nodded sagely.
This seemed to justify
Their actions and to thus condone
Each lover's roving eye.

The king said, 'We will entertain
The ladies now we're set,
And with good luck – who knows, we may
Gain their affection yet.'

Berowne said, 'Let the revels start –
We'll pass some merry hours.
Let true love run her tender course;
We'll strew her path with flowers.'

~ ~ ~

And so the king and his three lords
Attend the ladies fair,
And they enjoy great revelry
And partying once there.

But then a messenger arrives
Which ruins fun and dance,
Because he brings the gravest news
About the King of France.

The poor old king has passed away,
The monarch now is dead.
'Oh my beloved father, dear!'
His grieving daughter said.

The princess must return at once
And, though borne down with pain,
She thanks the king for giving back
The much loved Aquitaine.

The men, on seeing they're to leave
Swear to the heavens above
Their actions weren't just fun and games —
Then they avow their love.

The princess turned to face the king,
Upon her cheek one tear.
She said, 'I'll mourn my father now
Until this time next year.

'If for that time – you will agree
To be just on your own,
Remote from pleasure and all fun,
And live your life alone...

'And if when this twelve months have past
You still feel much the same,
Then I will be your loving wife;
I'll take, Navarre, your name.

'We will then live as king and queen.'
Then, with no backward glance,
She climbed onto her trusty steed
And set off home to France.

The lords too watched their ladies
Depart in the same way,
And they could only hope that they'd
Come back to them one day.

For they would have to wait the year,
Alone, what e'er the cost,
To find if they had won their loves
Or were 'Love's Labour's Lost?'

'If that's your wish,' said Ganymede

AS YOU LIKE IT

It doesn't always follow
That siblings will agree:
Sometimes the strife between them
Is clear for all to see.

It happens at all levels,
To rich and poor alike;
There is no way of telling
When jealousy will strike.

For once there was a famous duke
Who by unlucky chance,
Had a selfish brother
Who led him quite a dance.

For this mean brother, Frederick,
Full of nastiness and bile,
Stole his brother's dukedom by
Skulduggery and guile.

He kicked the duke, called Senior,
Out into the street
With just the clothes upon his back
And not a scrap to eat.

It's really hard to credit that
This man would stoop so low,
But truthfully it must be said
He wasn't nice to know.

The duke, thus driven from his court
So wickedly by force,
With just some faithful followers,
Set his unhappy course...

For Arden forest, lush and green,
Far from any town,
There to make some kind of life
And there to settle down.

This they did, and soon they saw
That there was much to please;
They liked the open air and found
They loved the life of ease.

No pomp and courtly customs
To bother them at all,
In fact they found life in the wood
Had power to enthral.

They savoured long, hot summer days;
They watched the dappled deer
Who – getting used to them – grew tame
And often grazed quite near.

So when they had to slaughter one
In order to get meat,
They all felt very sorry but
Of course, they had to eat.

And then the cold, dark winter came
With fierce and biting wind,
Their only barrier being hides
Of beasts that they had skinned.

The duke said, 'I can stand all this —
The winter's bitter mood —
But what I find so hard to take
Is gross ingratitude.

'The treachery of my brother
Is very hard to bear;
How could he take my dukedom?
How could he even dare?'

But then by moralising,
He'd do everything he could
To see the good in all around —
The blessings of the wood.

~ ~ ~

Duke Senior had a daughter
Who'd been retained at court,
For Frederick, the usurper,
Had had a selfish thought.

He'd make the daughter, Rosalind,
Remain — so she could be
A friend to his own daughter
And keep her company.

The girls ignored the quarrel
Between their fathers there;
They still remained the best of friends
Despite the warring pair.

Frederick's daughter, Celia,
Was very kind and good,
For she had tried so hard to do
The very best she could...

To make poor Rosalind happy
When her face wore a frown;
She tried to lift sad Rosalind
When she was feeling down.

~ ~ ~

And then one day as Celia
Was trying hard to bury
All young Rosalind's sad thoughts
And make her blithe and merry...

A message came from Frederick –
It came with all dispatch –
Asking if the girls would like
To see a wrestling match.

Although it seems unladylike
For them to watch such sport,
Wrestling was a pastime loved
By everyone at court.

So off they went most eagerly
To see this bloody sight;
It seemed to promise it would be
A most diverting fight.

The coming bout was to be fought
By two men badly matched;
To look at them it seemed that one
Would quickly be dispatched.

A powerful and massive man
Had just that day been billed
To fight a youth, whom all there thought
Was certain to be killed.

For he had no experience –
And though so bold of heart –
He hardly knew a thing about
The ancient wrestling art.

His opponent, it was said,
Was deadly to behold;
He'd slain so many in the ring
And knocked a lot out cold.

When Frederick saw the girls arrive
He said, 'Now you've appeared
I beg you speak to that young man,
Tell him we're all afeared...

'That he'll be slaughtered here today;
To fight would be unwise.
We have no wish to see him die
Right here before our eyes.'

So Celia addressed the youth,
She said, 'I beg you sir,
Please do not risk your life like this.'
He took no heed of her.

Then Rosalind herself spoke up
In kind and gentle way;
'Resist this madness, dear kind sir,
And do not fight I pray.'

His eyes met hers and in a flash
A love began to grow,
But in a still determined tone
He said, 'My answer's "no".

'I'm sorry to displease you both,
Two ladies, fine and fair,
And I am grateful for the fact
You choose to show such care.

'Give me your gentle wishes
And if I die right here,
Do not lament my passing,
I beg, be of good cheer...

'For if I'm killed, then so be it;
I'm not afraid,' he said.
"Twould be of little consequence
If I should end up dead.

'And if I lose my life today
No friends will grieve for me,
For I've no friends in all the world,
Nor loving family.

'And the space my body takes
Within this world,' he said,
'Can be far better filled, I'm sure
By someone else instead.'

~ ~ ~

The wrestling match got under way.
Rosalind, for her part –
So moved by what the youth had said –
Completely lost her heart.

The youth fought well and bravely
And in truth it must be said,
The kindly words from both the girls
Spun round inside his head.

It gave him strength and courage that
He didn't know he had,
And so he fought incredibly
For an untutored lad.

He quickly gained the upper hand
To everyone's surprise,
And then before the startled crowd –
Yes, right before their eyes...

He knocked the expert wrestler down,
Stretched him upon the floor;
He was completely out of it,
The man could fight no more.

Frederick jumped onto his feet,
'Bravo, young sir,' he yelled.
Nobody there could quite believe
The expert had been felled.

Frederick had the kindly thought
To take the youth in care,
Because he liked the lad he saw
All breathless, standing there.

'What is your name?' asked Frederick.
'Orlando,' he replied,
'Sir Rowland de Boys' youngest son,'
He said with quiet pride.

Frederick's face became a mask,
It went a ghostly white;
His tender feeling for the youth
Now quickly turned to spite.

His banished brother, Senior,
Had been Sir Rowland's friend,
Until the bold Sir Rowland
Had met a sorry end.

Frederick hated hearing
Any reference to that name,
But still the valour of the youth
Impressed him all the same.

So as he left in angry mood
Reflecting on his brother,
He said, 'Orlando, how I wish
That you were someone other.'

Rosalind was kinder though;
She was so pleased to hear
Orlando was the son of one
Her father held so dear.

Orlando was astounded
By Frederick's remark;
It seemed unkind, unwarranted,
Extremely cruel and stark.

But Rosalind and Celia both
Spoke to Orlando thus;
'We're sorry that Duke Frederick
Made such an awful fuss.'

Rosalind took a golden chain
From round her neck and said,
'Wear this, good sir, I beg you.'
Then placed it o'er his head.

~ ~ ~

When the girls were on there own,
Asked Celia, 'Is it true,
That you now love Orlando?
Perhaps he loves you too.'

Before her friend could answer
Or utter any more,
Duke Frederick came crashing in
And slammed the chamber door.

Sir Rowland as we've heard, had been
Duke Senior's favourite friend,
And thinking of the pair of them
Made Frederick descend...

Into the depths of black despair,
Because he felt for sure
The people loved the banished duke –
At least, from what he saw.

They favoured Rosalind as well,
Felt sorry for her too;
They pitied all her suffering
And all that she'd been through.

So now his hate boiled over –
On Rosalind it fell.
'Leave the court today,' he cried,
'You're banished now as well.'

Celia pleaded with him,
'Oh father, change your mind,
For I will miss dear Rosalind,
Please don't be so unkind.'

'Don't be a little fool,' he yelled,
'For all the time she stays,
The people love her more than you,
They much prefer her ways.

'When she is gone, you will appear
Much better than before.
I'll not relent, my mind's made up,
Don't argue anymore.'

Now Celia was a decent girl,
And loyal, good and true.
She said to Rosalind, 'Don't fret –
I'll come along with you.'

~ ~ ~

That night the two young girls crept out
Through the palace garden:
They went to join the banished duke
Among the trees of Arden.

Before they went, young Celia said,
'I think it would be wise,
For safety's sake, to make our trip
Dressed up in a disguise.'

They put on simple country clothes
To carry out their plan;
Celia dressed in woman's garb,
Rosalind as a man.

They'd tell everyone they met
They shared the selfsame mother,
They were a dear devoted pair,
A sister with her brother.

They called themselves by different names
To aid their little game:
Rosalind chose Ganymede,
Aliena, Celia's name.

They asked the court Fool, Touchstone,
'Are you prepared to be
Our travelling companion
To keep us company?'

He agreed – in truth he was
Quite under Celia's thumb.
He said, 'I'll follow where you go,
I shall be glad to come.'

The three set off for Arden –
A long way it was too –
And how to find Duke Senior,
They really had no clue.

When they finally arrived,
Tired out, quite on their knees,
Celia said, 'I've had it,
Let's rest beneath these trees.'

As they rested there awhile
A shepherd walked close by;
'Where can we find some food and rest?'
Asked Rosalind with a sigh.

The man was kind, 'My master
Will help you both,' he said.
'He has a cottage you can use –
He'll give you meat and bread.'

They gratefully accepted –
They'd stay there for a while
Until they found Duke Senior
Who'd free them from their trial.

~ ~ ~

We'll leave the girls right there for now,
As it is time to know
The fate of the courageous lad
Whose name was Orlando.

He's also in the forest,
So let's go back a trace,
In order to explain just how
He turned up in that place.

Orlando had a brother,
First of Sir Rowland's boys,
Who, when the old man passed away,
Soon set about his ploys.

His father had told this brother,
'Oliver, I charge you
To care for young Orlando
When my old life is through.

'Give him an education,
Watch over him, be true.
I trust your noble nature,
For I depend on you.'

But when Sir Rowland sadly died,
Oliver said, 'A fool,
Would waste his money on this kid
By sending him to school.'

But even though untutored,
Orlando soon became
A fine and decent person,
Most worthy of his name.

And for this reason, Oliver
Grew jealous of the lad;
The way he used Orlando would
Have made their father mad.

Oliver had put him up
To fight the fearsome guy
Whose hands had been the ones to cause
So many men to die.

He'd arranged the match and hoped
Orlando would be killed.
Imagine how annoyed he was
His wish was not fulfilled.

Orlando was victorious!
Oh, what a great surprise,
That he should win when set against
A man of such great size.

Oliver's anger overflowed –
'I'll sort him out for sure.
I'll burn his lodgings while he sleeps
And barricade his door.'

'Twas lucky for Orlando
That Oliver was heard
By one good, faithful servant
Who noted every word.

This servant's name was Adam and
He told him of the plan.
'You must leave right now,' he said,
'Get going while you can.'

Orlando left the house at once
And Adam followed too;
Running off just seemed to be
The safest thing to do.

They fled to Arden forest
But on arriving there,
So short they were of food and rest
It was too much to bear.

For Adam spoke of dying,
He was close to giving up.
'I need some food to eat,' he cried,
'And something good to sup.'

Orlando went in search of food
And entering a glade,
He saw a band of merry men
Who had a banquet laid.

It was Duke Senior and his men.
Orlando drew his sword,
He didn't think they'd give him food
Of their own accord.

He felt he'd have to steal to eat,
Thus his aggressive mood,
But the duke with kindness said,
'Sit down and have some food.'

Orlando sighed, 'Before I eat
There's one who's hungry too;
A poor old man who's come with me
Must eat before I do.'

The duke said, 'Fetch him instantly.'
Orlando disappeared.
And when he'd gone the duke remarked,
'How often life is weird.

'Such grim and woeful pageants
Before us are unfurled,
Like shows within the playhouses
Performed across the world.'

Jaques – one of his bravest men,
Who thought himself a sage,
Declared, 'Without a trace of doubt
All the world's a stage.

'And men and women players
On their respective stages,
And each man in his time plays parts,
To suit his seven ages.

'First he plays the infant
Who's wont to puke and mewl,
Then the whining boy who creeps
Unwillingly to school.

'Next he plays the lover,
Full of sighs and woes,
Then the soldier, bold and brave,
As off to war he goes.

'Then he acts the serious man,
Wise words and gross fat belly,
Then he shrinks and his meek voice
Is wobbly, like jelly.

'Second childhood – final scene –
Approaches with great haste,
It brings on mere oblivion:
No teeth, no eyes, no taste!'

~ ~ ~

Now Rosalind and Celia,
Who were settled in the wood –
Kept seeing carvings on the trees
They little understood.

They saw these carvings everywhere,
On trees, both far and wide,
And passionate love poems
On twigs were also tied.

The carvings spelt out 'Rosalind',
The poems were addressed
To Rosalind, and in them all
The author there professed...

She was the sweetest maiden
That he had ever known,
And in his breast, a fervent love
Had recently been sown.

As they pondered on the words
One fine and sunny day,
They came upon Orlando who
Was passing by that way.

He of course saw 'Ganymede',
A handsome looking male,
And Aliena – a young maid –
Along the woodland trail.

He stopped to pass the time of day,
For little did he think
That here was Rosalind, on whom
He'd used up so much ink.

Rosalind's young heart beat fast
To see him once again,
But still she thought it would be wise
If she were to refrain...

From saying who she really was –
So all she said was this:
'Have you observed the carvings?
They're very hard to miss!

'They're everywhere you chance to look –
I tell you, my good sir,
This lover must love Rosalind,
He surely dotes on her.

'He has a silly sickness, though
I'm sure his love is pure;
He needs some help to handle it,
I could suggest a cure.

'For if I knew just who he was,
I'd help him to recover.'
Orlando there and then confessed,
'I am this sorry lover.'

Rosalind (or Ganymede)
Said, 'This I now propose:
Come to our cottage every day
And there I will disclose...

'The way to cure this love of yours,
For I'll pretend to be
The lovely lady Rosalind;
You'll speak of love to me.

'And as your yearning words thus flow
I'll listen while you speak,
And sympathise most earnestly
With everything you seek.

'I'll act the love-shy maiden –
It won't take long, you'll see,
Before you feel ashamed of love,
And this will set you free.

'You'll rail against a lover's path
And you will quickly say
That this is not the road for you –
You'll want another way.'

Orlando had but little faith
In this, her remedy,
But said, 'I'll come along and try,
I'm sure it can't hurt me.'

He liked this young and pleasant lad –
In fact he thought he looked
Quite like the lady Rosalind
By whom he had been hooked.

And so from that day onward
Orlando made his way
Unto the shepherd's cottage
And practised what to say...

To his beloved Rosalind;
Used all those silly words
That lovers whisper all the time –
They were like courting birds.

And he loved every moment, though
He thought it just a game;
It was such fun for him to say
His Rosalind's fair name.

He also liked to speak aloud
(Not knowing in her sight)
All those little compliments
In which young men delight.

Of course he didn't realise
The one whom he addressed
Was Rosalind – for all the world
He never would have guessed.

Orlando had told Rosalind,
'Duke Senior lives quite near.'
Yet she had not rushed off to see
The father she held dear.

And then one day while walking
Along a path she knew,
She bumped into her father
Who said, 'How do you do?'

He didn't recognise her,
And so he said to her,
'Pray tell me of your parentage.'
She said, 'My gracious sir...

'I come from a good family
That's well known to be fine,
And so I think it's fair to say
I'm born of noble line...

'As noble as yourself,' she said,
In bold immodest style.
Her answer quite amused the duke,
He could not help but smile.

'To think this shepherd boy believes
He has a pedigree
That can compare with mine,' he thought,
'That really couldn't be.'

When Rosalind saw her father
Was fit and all aglow,
She thought, 'I'll wait a day or two
Before I let him know...

'That I am also in the wood,
There is no rush to tell.
I shall explain all in good time
How I am here and well.'

~ ~ ~

One day Orlando, setting off
To see his Ganymede,
Came suddenly upon a man
Asleep but in dire need.

A large green snake had come along
And found a way to wind
Its body round the poor man's neck,
And thus it was entwined.

But at the youth's approach the snake
Had quickly taken fright:
It slid away into a bush
And disappeared from sight.

You'd think that this was bad enough
But there was worse to come,
For what Orlando now perceived
Made all his limbs go numb.

A lioness was crouching
In the bushes there close by;
It seemed the sleeping man for sure
Was destined now to die.

The lioness was waiting for
The man to come awake,
For when he woke, well this would be
The time that she would make...

A swift and murderous attack
With one almighty leap,
For lioness's won't destroy
Their prey while it's asleep.

Orlando stood there mesmerised,
He felt his bold heart race,
And then he looked down at the man
And gazed into his face.

The person sleeping on the ground
Clearly was no other
Than someone whom we've met before:
Orlando's wicked brother!

It was the awful Oliver.
Orlando sighed a sigh –
'Perhaps I should just leave him here
And let the tyrant die.'

But brotherly affection
Came rushing to the fore;
All thoughts of leaving him to die
Went flying out the door.

He drew his sword, the lioness
Fought with great gnashing jaws,
And then it caught Orlando's arm
And tore him with its claws.

And blood rushed from the wound, but he
Began to fight again,
And thrust his sword with such great force,
The lioness was slain.

The noise made Oliver wake up;
He saw the awful sight:
His brother and the lioness
Engaged in mortal fight.

He saw that brave Orlando
Had risked his life to save
A scheming, worthless brother,
A coward and a knave.

Once the lioness was dead
He called his brother's name;
Borne down with great remorse he was –
And overpowering shame.

He repented there and then
His conduct in the past;
He now embraced his brother while
His tears flowed thick and fast.

Orlando was quite overjoyed
And readily forgave;
His brother thanked him for his life,
He said, 'You were so brave.'

And from that moment onward
Their affection grew and grew;
They put aside all quarrelling
And they began anew.

Then as he held Orlando close,
He said – with much alarm –
'Look here, you're badly wounded,
We must bind up your arm.'

Orlando said, 'I feel quite weak,
So while I rest, I ask
If you will do a favour, and
Perform a little task.

'Please go and tell friend Ganymede
I cannot come today.'
Oliver said of course he'd go
And hurried on his way.

He reached the woodland cottage, where
He said, 'I've come to tell
That your good friend Orlando
Isn't feeling well.'

He recounted everything:
How brave Orlando fought,
And how despite his own cruel ways –
The selfish end he'd sought...

Orlando had forgiven him.
He said, 'How I regret
The way I've wronged my brother, and
I will not soon forget...

'How freely he forgave me,
And put my wrong aside.'
Celia, as she listened, found
That she could barely hide...

The way she was beginning
To fall in love, right there,
With Oliver, who showed remorse
And genuine despair.

Rosalind, when she was told
Orlando had been hurt
Collapsed right there upon the floor
In all the muck and dirt.

It seemed most strange that this young man
Should swoon upon the floor;
When Rosalind came round, she said,
'It was pretence, no more.'

~ ~ ~

When Oliver returned again
To where Orlando lay,
He found his spirits had revived
For he was quick to say...

'I feel a whole lot better from
The peace of this kind wood,
For resting here a while has done
An awful lot of good.'

Oliver on hearing this
Just couldn't wait and said,
'I've fallen for a shepherd girl
And now I hope to wed.'

Orlando said, 'I counsel you
Most strongly, do not tarry –
Ask the lady for her hand
And then you two can marry.'

When later all was settled,
To gentle Ganymede
Orlando said, 'Would Rosalind
Were here so I could plead...

'Her hand in holy marriage;
For her to be my wife.
I swear it is the only thing
I really want from life.'

'If that's your wish,' said Ganymede,
'Then put away your sorrow;
I'll arrange for you to wed
Fair Rosalind tomorrow.'

Orlando, very doubtful,
Thought it a joke – just play,
That Ganymede was acting in
A rather silly way.

But Ganymede insisted
That Rosalind he'd wed.
'I'll use some magic that I've learnt
And bring her here,' he said.

~ ~ ~

The following day they gathered,
With everyone excited.
The duke was there as well, of course,
For he had been delighted...

When told his daughter would appear –
Oh, what a great surprise!
But he suspected Ganymede
Might just be telling lies.

Then Ganymede said to the duke,
'My lord, I wish to know,
Would you agree for Rosalind
To marry Orlando?'

The duke replied, 'Oh, that I would.'
And Ganymede then said,
'Orlando, would you too consent
To also being wed?'

'With all my heart,' came his reply.
Then Ganymede withdrew,
Removed her man's attire – became
The Rosalind they knew.

She didn't linger very long,
She did not keep them guessing;
When she returned she knelt and asked
Her father for his blessing.

They had a double wedding –
There seemed no time to lose,
And then a messenger arrived
Who brought them joyful news.

Frederick did now repent
The error of his ways,
And made a declaration
That he would spend his days...

In a religious order.
He said, 'When I get there,
I'll kneel in contemplation and
Devote myself to prayer.'

The first act of his penitence
Was forthwith to return
The dukedom to his brother;
And then he would adjourn...

To life in lone seclusion –
And do so with all speed.
Oh, what a fine result this was!
What splendid news indeed!

Thus all was for the better –
'As you like it', you might say.
For everyone prefers it when
A tale turns out this way.

*'Why tell her of my passion,
And of my love,'* he said

TWELFTH NIGHT

One fine day in Messaline
Right in the early dawn,
With but an hour between them
Identical twins were born.

One twin was a little boy,
Sebastian was his name;
The girl was called Viola –
The children looked the same.

And as they grew to be adults,
The sister and the brother
Still looked alike – you couldn't tell
One twin from the other.

Just like two peas within a pod,
Like cherries on a tree,
The pair were quite identical
As far as one could see.

~ ~ ~

Now we'll miss their happy childhood
And very quickly skip
To a day when they are taking
A voyage on a ship.

Their vessel hit a heavy storm,
Was tossed and thrown amok,
Until the huge and mighty waves
Drove it onto a rock.

Most of the wretched souls on board
Were drowned in watery graves;
A few though struggled to a boat
And fought the mighty waves.

Among them was the captain,
Viola and some crew;
And when they reached the shore they were
Tired and soaked right through.

'It's so hard to be thankful,'
Viola quietly said,
'Not when I fear my brother
Is very likely dead.'

The captain answered bravely,
'Now don't give up so fast,
I'm sure I saw him clinging to
A piece of broken mast.'

Viola then began to hope
Her brother might survive,
There seemed at least a slender chance
He might still be alive.

She wondered then what she could do
In this so foreign land,
And asked the kindly captain
If he would lend a hand.

'Do you know this place?' she asked.
'Illyria,' he said.
'Why it was very close to here
That I was born and bred.'

'Please can you tell me also
The ruler of this place?'
'A noble duke,' was his reply,
'Known for his charm and grace.

'His name is Duke Orsino,
He's loved both far and wide,
Yet he remains a bachelor,
He's never found a bride.

'But that was now a month ago,
'Twas then I last came here,
And at that time there was much talk
Of one he holds most dear.

'The lady's called Olivia –
They say he loves her so –
She is the daughter of a count
Who died twelve months ago.

'She lived then with her brother,
But he died and so since then,
She's lived alone in mourning
And will not speak to men.'

Viola shared the selfsame fate
As this unknown other –
In that she also mourned the loss
Of a dear, close brother.

She thought perhaps that she could live
With this unhappy soul,
So asked the good sea captain
To help attain this goal.

He said he couldn't help her,
All who went received rebuke.
'Olivia won't see you –
She won't even see the duke.'

Viola knew that she must work
So hatched another plan,
To be the Duke Orsino's page
By dressing as a man.

For her to put on male attire
Would be most strange indeed,
But in this place – all on her own –
It might help her succeed.

The captain had been kind to her,
She judged him to be fair.
She told him what she planned to do
And then she made him swear...

To keep her project secret,
Which he said he would do,
And then she asked him for his help
To guide the whole plan through.

For she would need men's clothing –
Which he thought very funny,
But still he said he'd help her so
She counted out some money.

He hurried off to buy the clothes –
She told him to take care
To buy the kind of garments
Her brother used to wear.

Once she was dressed in men's attire
She looked just like her brother:
In fact, 'twould be impossible
To tell one from the other.

And then the captain helped her
Achieve the goal she sought
By having her presented
At Duke Orsino's court.

She said, 'My name's Cesario' –
And so it was, her plan,
Had instantly succeeded as
They took her for a man.

The duke was kind just as she'd heard
And handsome too, forsooth;
For his part he was most impressed
With this good-looking youth.

He took Viola as his page,
Which filled her with elation,
And she did all things to fulfil
The duties of her station.

~ ~ ~

Viola was attentive and
Devoted to her lord;
She soon became his favourite,
His appreciation soared.

One day Orsino told her,
His features creased by frowns,
How he adored Olivia
Despite the ups and downs.

How she refused to love him and
She wouldn't let him call;
She wouldn't even write or now
Communicate at all.

Viola heard his story –
But it's a risky matter,
To wait upon a bold young duke
And share his idle chatter.

For now she found she loved him with
A love that was as true
As his was for Olivia:
Of course – he had no clue.

She let him speak – then asked him,
'If a maid loved you my lord,
But there was just no way you felt
Of similar accord...

'You'd tell her it was hopeless.
Your heart could not be earned.
That it was quite impossible
Her love could be returned.'

The duke said that no lady
Could love in the same way
That he loved fair Olivia
Each moment of the day.

Viola said a woman's heart
Could equally be true;
She spoke with lively passion,
For this of course she knew.

The duke said, 'Come, Cesario,
What know you of womankind?
How can you understand the things
That go on in their mind?'

As he spoke, Viola found
She loved him even more –
But at this point a messenger
Appeared there at the door.

He'd come back from Olivia –
He'd been sent by the duke –
And from his face Orsino knew
He brought a fresh rebuke.

'My lord,' the messenger began,
'I'm very much afraid
You will not like the message here,
Given by her maid.

'Her mistress will on no account
Let any see her face;
She says it shall be shrouded by
A veil of opaque lace.

'And will remain unlooked at
Till seven years go by.'
When good Orsino heard these words
He sighed a heavy sigh.

'Oh what a fine heart she must have,
Truer than any other,
That she can pay this debt of love
For her departed brother!

'If she suffers for her sibling
In this tremendous way,
Why how she'll love if Cupid's dart
Should strike her one fine day.'

And then he said to Viola,
'Oh, you must now depart,
And take to fair Olivia
The secrets of my heart.

'Insist on gaining entry.'
She said, 'And if I do,
What can I add to all the things
That she has heard from you?'

'Why tell her of my passion,
And of my love,' he said,
'Tell her how strongly I desire
The two of us be wed.'

~ ~ ~

So Viola set off in haste,
Although inclined to tarry,
For now she wooed another for
The man *she* wished to marry.

She did her duty as he asked –
She could resist no more –
And very soon she found herself
Outside Olivia's door.

She asked then for the lady,
Said she had things to tell;
The servant said her mistress
Just wasn't feeling well.

With haste Viola answered,
'What I must say won't keep.'
The servant then responded,
'My lady's fast asleep.'

Viola was determined that
She should not call in vain,
And so she sent the servant to
Olivia again.

At last the lady yielded to
Viola's persistence,
Which, in truth, had broken down
Olivia's resistance.

She said she'd listen once again
To Orsino's loving plea –
But warned, 'This bold new messenger
Will have no luck with me.'

Viola, entering the room,
Addressed her in this way,
'Are you the fair Olivia?
Tell me the truth, I pray.

'I would not waste my precious words
On anyone but her.'
Olivia graciously replied,
'I'm whom you seek, good sir.'

'Then please remove, I beg of you,
That white mysterious veil.'
Olivia did as she was asked –
She rather liked this male.

Pangs of desire were growing
That she could not assuage
For this young man who she believed
Was but a humble page.

Now Viola wished to get a glimpse
Of every tiny feature,
Of this sad lady whom the duke
Thought such a lovely creature.

She knew Orsino loved her
Throughout his very being,
But Viola thought her beauty
Lay only in the seeing.

'You are most fair,' she whispered,
'It's little wonder why
The Duke Orsino loves you –
A feast for any eye.'

Olivia answered gravely,
'You're gracious and most kind,
But noble Duke Orsino
Knows all too well my mind.

'Though he is good and valiant,
This I most surely know:
I really cannot love him –
He knew this long ago.

'Tell him I cannot care for him,
Tell him he must refrain
From sending further messengers –
Unless *you* come again.'

Viola then departed
To tell what had occurred,
And when she'd gone, Olivia
Mused over every word.

She wished that this Cesario
Had been himself the duke,
But at this thought she gave herself
A half-amused rebuke.

She cursed herself for feeling thus,
But fast as this thought came
She just as fast excused herself,
As folk will do, from blame.

She just ignored the gap in wealth
Between her and the page,
And she forgot her strong reserve
And let affection rage.

She wanted young Cesario
And did a reckless thing;
She told her servant, 'Follow him,
And give him this gold ring.'

The servant was then told to ask
Had it been left behind?
Was it a present from the duke?
If so 'twas very kind...

But she could not accept it.
'Twas graciously returned,
For gifts of such high value
Should always be well earned.

Olivia hoped the page would see
From this contrived device
That she was now in love with him,
Not merely being nice.

Viola guessed the truth at once,
Not knowing of the ring,
She clearly saw how matters stood –
It was the weirdest thing.

She saw her master's lady
Was now in love with her,
It was the very strangest thing
That ever could occur.

'Alas!' poor Viola cried out,
'Things are not what they seem.
The sorrowing Olivia
Has fallen for a dream.

'For my disguise has caused her sigh
These fruitless sighs for me,
As I do for Orsino –
Though neither love can be.'

~ ~ ~

Returning to Orsino
She found he paced the floor.
She said, 'Olivia firmly says,
Don't bother any more.'

The duke was still determined
That he would get his way;
He sent Cesario again
To try the following day.

Before he left the duke desired
A love song to be sung,
And noticed that Cesario –
A gentle boy and young...

Was most affected by the song.
It's soulful, sad refrain
Of deep and unrequited love,
Told of a lover's pain.

'Now on my life,' exclaimed the duke,
'Cesario, don't be coy,
Have you beheld a face you love?
Say honestly, my boy.'

Cesario declared he had.
Then said the duke, 'Tell me,
What kind of woman's caught your eye?
What kind of age is she?'

So to the object of her heart
She said with deep affection,
'My lord she is about your age
And has the same complexion.'

This made the duke smile broadly
To think this youthful page
Should love a dark-haired woman who
Was somewhere near *his* age.

~ ~ ~

Viola returned again –
Olivia made no fight
Because she thought the handsome page
A very welcome sight.

Viola tried, in her disguise,
Everything she could
To plead Orsino's case but still
Her pleading did no good.

Lady Olivia briskly said,
'I asked you to refrain
From speaking of the noble duke –
Don't mention him again.

'I'd much prefer a different suit.'
This was the plainest talk;
It was a road that Viola
Had just no wish to walk.

Olivia spoke again at length,
She truly spoke her mind,
She said that young Cesario was
The dearest love she'd find.

When on Viola's handsome face
Concern began to fashion,
She saw she was the victim of
An unrequited passion.

'I see contempt upon your face
Now I have let you know,
But still despite the way you feel
I truly love you so.'

But in vain the lady wooed.
Viola wished to leave,
She simply wanted to depart
And let Olivia grieve.

She said she would not come again
To plead Orsino's case,
Or ever love a woman, then
She hurried from that place.

Viola now consumed by guilt,
Thought, 'I've been very cruel.'
But then, as she walked down the street,
Was challenged to a dual.

She didn't recognise the man
Who was her persecutor,
But he had been Olivia's
One-time rejected suitor.

He was mad because he'd heard
Olivia loved a page;
The very thought had put him in
A fierce and towering rage.

What now could poor Viola do?
Fight on her own accord?
She was a helpless woman and
She couldn't use a sword.

Her rival then began to shout,
His sword was fully drawn,
She nearly then and there confessed
To being a woman born.

But then another stranger who
By chance was passing by –
Spoke as if he were a friend;
She'd no idea why.

'If this youth has caused offence,'
He said, 'I'll take the blame,
But if you cross your sword with me,
Take heed – 'twill be no game.'

Before she could enquire just why
He helped her in this way,
Two officers stopped her saviour
And had some words to say.

They said they'd come along and to
Arrest him then and there:
The stranger said to Viola,
'This really isn't fair.'

But still he was arrested for
What was an old offence.
He seemed unable to provide
A reasonable defence.

And then he said to Viola,
'I gave a purse to you.'
She wondered what all this could mean –
She didn't have a clue.

'Let me have the purse,' he said.
'I'll need some money now.
Please hand it over right away.'
She stood with furrowed brow.

'Why do you look surprised?' he asked.
Viola still looked fazed;
She said she didn't know him and
His words left her amazed.

Moreover she was adamant,
She'd never had his purse.
The stranger raved on angrily
And then began to curse.

'You utter such ungrateful words
With every single breath;
Was it not I who snatched you from
The very jaws of death?

'And it was me who gave my purse –
And now you stand and say,
You've never had the golden coins
I freely gave away.'

He spoke as if he knew her,
Not like a perfect stranger.
'For you, I travelled to this place,
And now I'm in great danger.

'You have been most disloyal
To one who was a friend.'
His words came tumbling angrily;
A torrent without end.

He called her 'good Sebastian',
Then, 'Sebastian' again;
Viola tried to quiz him but
Her words were all in vain.

For he was held there prisoner,
Although he cursed and raved:
Viola wondered if it was
Her twin whom he had saved.

She hoped he knew her brother,
(Which was in fact the case)
You will recall these noble twins
Each bore the selfsame face.

The stranger was a sailor,
Antonio by name,
And that he'd saved Sebastian's life
Was not an idle claim.

He'd found her brother drowning,
A victim of fatigue;
So this then was the answer to
This very strange intrigue.

Once he had saved Sebastian
From the raging storm,
The friendship then between the two
Became extremely warm.

He kept Sebastian company
Wherever he would go,
And that's what caused the muddle
Of which we already know.

Sebastian had been quite keen
To see Orsino's court;
Antonio, though, was known there for
A battle he'd once fought.

It was against Orsino's ships
So he knew – without fail,
If ever he returned he might
End up inside a jail.

But Antonio had decided
To take his chance and come,
To support Sebastian
Who was his closest chum.

He'd said, upon arrival,
'Take my purse – buy what you will.
I'll wait here at this comfy inn
Until you've shopped your fill.'

But when his friend did not return
At the appointed time,
He'd left the inn – and now had been
Arrested for his crime.

He had mistaken Viola
For Sebastian, it's true –
And that is why he'd boldly said,
'I'll fight this fight for you.'

And Viola, of course denied
She had Antonio's purse;
She said she didn't know him so
Things went from bad to worse.

The thought of such ingratitude
Is really very bad.
No wonder that Antonio
Was mortified and mad.

Antonio was led away.
Viola then took flight;
She wouldn't give the suitor chance
To pick another fight.

~ ~ ~

But then a short time later
Sebastian came along.
The suitor thought, 'That page again!'
Of course he was quite wrong.

He went straight for Sebastian,
Struck him a hefty blow;
Sebastian was quite amazed
But didn't let it show.

He simply drew his sword to fight –
But then who should come out?
Olivia – to find out what
The noise was all about.

She called, 'My dearest love, come here,
I beg you, quickly, do!'
Then turning to the suitor snapped,
'Begone! I don't want you.'

Sebastian was surprised to see
The care she chose to show,
But he was glad to thus escape
A foe he didn't know.

For her part fair Olivia was
Ecstatically inclined
To think that young Cesario
Had come to change his mind.

No sign of disenchantment
Showed on his handsome face,
And of his former coolness
There really was no trace.

Sebastian was quite relaxed,
And took it in good part,
He thought her strange but just supposed
She had a kindly heart.

He saw she was the mistress
Of all that she surveyed,
And when she showed she loved him – well,
His heart was quickly swayed.

She thought that her Cesario,
For such he seemed to be,
Was in a most receptive mood
So said, 'Please marry me.'

Sebastian declared he would –
A priest came right away,
And they were married there and then;
She would not brook delay.

Of course Sebastian wanted
To tell Antonio;
He said, 'I'll go and fetch him.
I can't wait to let him know.'

Sebastian then hurried off.
'I won't be long,' he said,
'Antonio won't believe me when
I tell him I am wed.'

~ ~ ~

The duke arrived then on the scene
With Viola at his side.
The officer approached and said,
'This rogue here must be tried.'

He brought in poor Antonio,
In chains – who quickly saw
Viola with Orsino
Outside Olivia's door.

He thought, 'There's my Sebastian.'
And cried, now feeling glad,
'This is my friend – he'll vouch for me.'
The duke thought he was mad.

'Three months ago,' he carried on,
'I saved this youth at sea.'
The duke replied with great disdain,
'*Then*, he was *here* with me.'

Appearing then, Olivia,
Saw Viola and said,
'Cesario, my darling!'
Viola turned bright red.

The duke on hearing these fond words
Flew into a rage,
He said, 'Come here you wretched boy,
You most unfaithful page.'

Olivia called out after them,
'Cesario, I'm your wife.'
Viola cried, 'Not so – I love
The duke more than my life.'

Olivia then stopped them.
'This honest priest,' she said,
'Will vouch that dear Cesario
And I have just got wed.'

Her words cut through Orsino with
The sharpness of a knife,
He found it hard to credit that
She was his page's wife.

He realised with anguish
His greatest love had wed,
And turning to Cesario,
'Out of my sight!' he said.

The course that things had taken
Was as Viola feared,
But at this point her double
Unexpected, reappeared.

It was her lost Sebastian
Who came upon the scene,
Whereat they all looked quite amazed –
What could this marvel mean?

The twins were truly overjoyed
To find once more each other;
He hugged his sister warmly,
She kissed her long lost brother.

So everything was now explained –
Olivia then said,
'It seems I've loved a woman but
I'll love her twin instead.'

So with Olivia now wed
All hopes of her must die.
The duke, however, was well-known
To have a roving eye.

He thought about young Viola,
How lovely she had been;
He'd always thought Cesario was
The fairest page he'd seen.

He thought how she had often shown –
On many countless days –
How she adored and cared for him
In many different ways.

These thoughts revolving in his mind
He soon began to see
That she was meant for him – so said,
'Cesario, marry me.'

The duke still used the name that she
Had given from the start.
Viola looked at him and said,
'I will with all my heart.'

Olivia, on seeing that
Their love had blossomed, said
'Come, meet the priest right now and then
The two of you can wed.

'And also, Duke Orsino –
As I'm now wed for sure –
I hope you will accept me as
Your dear sister-in-law.'

The duke then readily agreed
To everything she said,
Then turning to Viola
He gently bowed his head.

'My dear, you've called me master
Through all my pain and strife,
But here I give my hand and say
Please be your master's wife.'

And so it was, these siblings both
Were married in this way,
Twin brother and twin sister tied
The knot the selfsame day:

And it is true, that neither twin
Would have lost their heart,
If their ship had not been wrecked–
And torn the pair apart.

So everyone was overjoyed
And we are pleased to say,
Antonio was pardoned
Upon that happy day.

*He says, 'Has any soldier
Still got the nerve to fight?'*

TROILUS AND CRESSIDA

War is such an awful thing,
So many people die,
And often soldiers can't recall –
They can't remember why...

They're fighting every single day;
What they are battling for?
What started it at first – indeed
The reason for the war?

Thus it was in this our tale,
Greek soldiers all had tramped
To Troy – and there for seven years,
Their forces had encamped.

For all these years they had fought on –
Attack then re-attack;
And as the Greeks besieged great Troy,
The Trojans fought them back.

Whatever was the reason
For this protracted war?
Why were the Greeks so thus intent –
What were they fighting for?

Well Priam, who was King of Troy,
Had three sons he adored;
They were brave and brash and bold
And all could use a sword.

The oldest was called Hector,
Paris was another,
And Troilus —who loved Cressida —
He was the youngest brother.

Now seven weary years before,
Paris of Troy had done
A deed that Greeks both near and far —
In fact just everyone...

Believed to be the meanest act.
This selfish, horrid boy
Had stolen beauteous Helen and
Had taken her to Troy.

Menelaus was her spouse —
The King of Sparta — so
It's not surprising that the Greeks
Made up their minds to go...

To Troy and there besiege the town;
The actions of the lad
Had got the Greeks in angry mood;
Oh, they were really mad.

And so the Greeks had come to Troy
Intent to get her back,
And this then was the reason for
The seven year attack.

~ ~ ~

Now Troilus was the brother
Of naughty Paris there,
And he is desperately in love
With Cressida, so fair.

He says, 'I'm sick of fighting,
I want to take a wife;
I want to settle down and start
To live a normal life.

'I'm tired of living in a place
Where only fighting rules;
As far as I'm concerned they're all
A bunch of silly fools.'

So he decides he'll have a try
To win the maiden's hand;
He wants to give the lovely girl
A shiny wedding band.

But in those ancient days of yore
It wasn't the done thing
To propose, 'Please marry me –
And here's a wedding ring.'

It happened in a special way –
For if a youth was keen,
His courting was done for him by
A trusted go-between.

And so he asked his uncle –
Pandarus was his name –
If he would go and carry out
The age-old wooing game.

'Tell her how much I love her;
That she's the one for me.'
His uncle said, 'Don't worry lad
I'll sort this out, you'll see.'

So Pandarus made his way
To Cressida right there,
And said, 'My nephew Troilus
Will wither in despair...

'If you refuse to love him,
If you deny his suit.'
Pandarus then began to think
There might be a dispute...

For she looked down her nose at him,
Seemed cool and very coy,
And said she thought young Troilus
Was just a silly boy.

But then with more persuasion
She blurted out the truth,
And said she thought that Troilus
Was quite a handsome youth.

And then she came right out with it
And said, 'I must tell you
His true love isn't wasted –
For I love Troilus too.'

'Then come along,' said Pandarus,
'To Troilus right away.'
And she spent loving time with him
For all of that long day.

And they professed their passion,
And each said, 'I love you.'
And you would think you could be sure
That they would both be true!

~ ~ ~

The Greeks who're camped outside the walls
Are sitting down to sup,
And almost every one of them
Is feeling quite fed up.

They've had enough of this long war,
And Ulysses then says,
'We've been here for far too long –
More than two thousand days.'

And there within the city,
Behind the walls of Troy,
They're fed up with it all as well;
There isn't too much joy.

'It's surely true,' then Hector says.
'Helen has caused such woe.
Let's give her to the Greeks – just let
The silly woman go.

'She's not worth all this trouble,
She's caused us so much pain,
Let's give her back and then enjoy
Some peace here once again.

'Why, it would be so easy,
For all we'd have to say
Is, here take Helen off our hands,
Take her back today.'

But Troilus then spoke up and said,
'But what about those slain?
If we just give her back it means
That they all died in vain.'

And so they argued back and forth
With no conclusion made.
They didn't give fair Helen back,
But made another trade.

For Cressida is just about
To find her life turned round,
As all her plans for marriage
Are soon to run aground.

For she, who'd thought she'd surely be
A bride in just short weeks,
Now finds her father wishes her
To join him with the Greeks.

For he'd defected to their side
Many years before,
And now he wants his daughter there,
To be with him once more.

A deal is very quickly done:
The Greeks agree to trade
A prisoner for Cressida –
And thus a deal was made.

And so the Greeks then send a lad
To bring the young girl back.
He makes his way to Troy's great walls
Along a little track.

Diomedes was this lad's name –
A brave chap through and through.
Muscular and full of charm
And so good-looking too.

Cressida says a sad farewell
To Troilus standing there;
With teardrops welling in her eyes
She cries, 'I'll always care.

'There'll never be another love
In all my life but you,
And when I'm taken far away
I'll not know what to do.'

And so with tender kisses
The two young lovers part;
Each vows the other always
Will own their loving heart.

And Troilus there and then avows,
'Somehow I'll find a way
To creep into the Grecian camp
And see you every day.'

The lovelorn lass now follows
The strong and handsome lad,
Back to the Greek encampment
To be with her old dad.

And as she follows this young man
The girl begins to feel,
That Troilus, whom she's left behind
Is really no big deal.

In fact she thinks, 'I like this lad.'
Oh, what a fickle wench!
We all thought leaving Troilus
Would be a massive wrench.

~ ~ ~

But now Prince Hector, who's a champ,
The finest fighter there,
Decides it would be jolly good
To set the Greeks a dare.

He challenges just any Greek
To come against his might.
He says, 'Has any soldier
Still got the nerve to fight?'

He thinks they'll send Achilles,
A fighter bold and cruel,
But this warrior's not inclined
To get into a duel.

He's Greece's bravest soldier –
In battle, such a sight –
But at this time he's sulking and
Won't leave his tent to fight.

His problem is that he is full
Of silly, childish pride.
He thinks he's not revered enough –
So in his tent does hide.

And so the Greeks sent Ajax,
But he is related
To Hector, so their fighting urge
Had very soon abated.

Hector cried, 'Let's call a truce.
We shouldn't fight each other.
After all you're close enough
To almost be my brother.'

And so the Greeks and Trojans too
Agreed a truce that night,
But on the morrow – all agreed –
They would resume the fight.

So they sat down to celebrate,
The Greeks and Trojans all.
It really was the strangest thing;
They really had a ball.

But then Achilles changed his mind
For he was quite hell-bent
On fighting – and so now he asked
Bold Hector to his tent.

He wished to size the Trojan up –
He was intent to know
If Hector really was the type
To make a worthy foe.

He told his friend Patroclus,
'I'll heat his blood tonight
With Grecian wine – tomorrow though
I'll cool it in a fight.'

Now Troilus who was also there,
Said, 'I'll now go and seek
My beloved Cressida.'
The thought made him feel weak.

And so he went a-searching,
And to his horror saw
His lover with the young Greek lad.
He cried out, 'Oh, you whore!

'Oh Cressida! Oh Cressida!
How could you be untrue!'
But the damage had been done
And this sad Troilus knew.

He vowed that when the fighting
Resumed the following day
He'd kill the fawning Grecian lad;
He'd kill him in the fray.

~ ~ ~

The next day when the sun appeared
And dawn burst through once more,
The Trojans and the Greeks again
Returned to bloody war.

True to his word, then Troilus
Sought Diomedes out.
They both fought hard – a stirring sight,
Of that there was no doubt.

But neither gained the upper hand.
There really was no way
That either would claim victory
On that particular day.

Then in the heat of battle
Achilles and Hector met;
The stage for a great struggle
Was well and truly set.

But after quite a short exchange
Of thrusts and blows and all,
Achilles, puffing hard, exclaimed,
'I'm too tired to brawl.

'So let us take a breather,
I'm really out of shape.'
And Hector, his opponent, then
Just let the Greek escape.

He could have overpowered him.
He could have won the day.
But Hector let Achilles go –
An act of great fair play.

Hector continued fighting,
His sword flew all around,
And many Grecian soldiers
He struck down to the ground.

And through that raging, crashing throng
Hector delivered death,
Until he said, 'My work is done.
I'll now regain my breath.

'My sword has had its fill today
Of blood and death and gore;
So for today I'll say "Enough",
And I will fight no more.'

But as he laid his sword aside,
Thus totally unarmed,
And certain in the knowledge that
He would remain unharmed...

Achilles came back on the scene:
He had a band of men –
His Myrmidons, his warriors –
He turned around and then...

Ignoring rules of chivalry,
Cried, 'Slaughter Hector here!'
And that is what they did, they killed
This man who knew no fear.

Then Achilles set about
A really awful thing;
A quite disgraceful act upon
The son of Troy's great king.

He tied the bleeding body
Of Hector, to his horse,
Then jumped astride the weary steed
And then he set his course...

Towards the massive walls of Troy:
Once there, he showed them all
How he had slain their much loved prince,
And what would thus befall...

Those who opposed Achilles –
There'd be a price to pay.
The Trojans to a man were stunned
By all they saw that day,

And for a moment some declared,
'Let us now end this war.'
But Troilus up and said he felt
That he was really sure...

That Hector's death should be avenged;
They couldn't let it go.
It was a coward's act, performed
By an unworthy foe.

So the fighting recommenced;
A moral's here for sure.
That violence begets violence
And keeps on causing war.

'*He sings her songs and praises her*'

ALL'S WELL THAT ENDS WELL

We start when old Count Roussillon
Has drawn his final breath;
His son and heir now takes his place
Upon the old man's death.

The King of France, he loved the count
And when he heard he'd died,
He called the young son, Bertram,
To join him at his side.

He wished to pass his favour from
The old count to the new;
What a really gracious thing
For such a king to do!

Of course this regal summons
With which Bertram had been blest,
Amounted to an order,
'Twas no polite request.

He had no choice but to attend,
He had to leave that day;
Nobody with an ounce of sense
Would choose to disobey.

His loving mum, the countess,
Was tortured by the thought
That her dear son was leaving,
And she was most distraught.

It was like a new bereavement –
Oh, what a rotten thing!
Just when she needed Bertram
He was summoned to the king.

The king's old henchman, Lord Lafeu –
When he'd been sent to call
Young Bertram to the king – had said,
'The king's not well at all.

'He has the strangest illness,
Its origin obscure;
His doctors all just scratch their heads –
They cannot find a cure.'

When the countess heard these words
She clasped her hands and said,
'A friend of mine knew medicine,
But sadly he's now dead.

'He was Gerard de Narbon,
A doctor of great skill,
Who – knowing he was dying –
Requested in his will...

'I care for his dear daughter;
This was his final plea.
I, of course, agreed at once,
And so she lives with me.'

Helena, the daughter,
Then began to cry.
The countess kept on talking, though
She did so with a sigh;

'She misses her poor father –
But tries so hard to please;
Such a lovely disposition
And worthy qualities.'

Bertram then stepped forward.
He said, 'It's time to go.
I'll miss you mother, very much
As I am sure you know.'

The countess said to Lord Lafeu,
'You look a decent sort,
So keep an eye on Bertram –
He's not used to life at court.'

Then Bertram said to Helena
In cool and measured way,
'Take care of my dear mother,
Look out for her, I pray.'

His manner was quite brusque and short
For little did he know
That when the lady cried, she wept
Because she loved *him* so.

Though mourning for her father,
Her tears fell all the more
For Bertram, who she now could see
Was walking out the door.

She'd loved him for a long, long time
But knew she held no worth
In his eyes – due to the fact
She was of humble birth.

He was of noble pedigree
And therefore way above
Poor Helena, who was quite sure
She'd never win his love.

For she was but a servant
And though her passion burned,
She knew it was impossible
That it would be returned.

~ ~ ~

So Bertram then departed –
Helena's love still shone.
In fact it burned more brightly,
Despite the fact he'd gone.

In silent moments on her own
The girl would slowly wander
Around the mansion, deep in thought,
And at these times she'd ponder...

Upon her love for Bertram and
The illness of the king,
Then she began to be convinced
Of a momentous thing.

'I'm sure I have the means to cure
His Majesty,' she thought,
'Contained within the remedies
That my poor father taught.

'A potion with amazing power
I know would hit the spot,
And very quickly prove a cure
For what the king has got.'

So she began to think she'd go
To Paris – to the king.
But then she thought, 'There's not a chance
He'd listen to a thing...

'For I am but a lowly girl;
This hill's too steep to climb.
I'd never get to speak to him –
To try would waste my time.'

A steward heard her talking
To herself like this one day.
He crouched in hiding and he heard
All that she had to say.

He caught her at a moment
Declaring to herself
Her love for Bertram, and her fear,
That she was on the shelf.

The steward told the countess;
Repeated every word
That through his secret watching
He'd slyly overheard.

The countess summoned Helena
When the day was done.
She said, 'Now tell me truthfully,
Do you adore my son?'

Embarrassed, Helena then blushed,
Her cheeks turned crimson red;
Her mind was working overtime –
'Do *you* love him?' she said.

The countess said, 'That's no reply!
Now, tell me how you feel.'
Helena found the questioning
A terrible ordeal.

'Speak up!' the countess yelled at her.
'Don't be evasive, girl.'
Poor Helena was lost for words,
Her thoughts were in a whirl.

But finally she spoke and said,
'Yes ma'am, I love your son,
And though I know I'm in the wrong,
For me, he is the one.

'I know our love can never be,
The social gap's too wide,
So I would never let him know
How I feel deep inside.'

The countess made no comment,
But she asked, 'Is it true
You plan to go to Paris?
And then what will you do?'

This was her aim, Helena said;
'I think that I can bring
Some succour and assistance,
And maybe cure the king.'

The countess uttered not a word –
Approval nor of blame –
But she was thinking that the girl
Might somehow make her name.

For if she cured the sickly king
There'd simply be no end
To his relief and gratitude;
He'd always be her friend.

And so the countess bid her go,
She wished her 'best of luck.'
Without a doubt she did admire
Her bravery and pluck.

~ ~ ~

When Helena reached Paris
She begged Lord Lafeu's aid,
And an appointment with the king
Was very quickly made.

When asked to take the potion
The king would not concur.
He said, 'I'll not take medicine
From one the likes of her.'

And though he was still feeling
Extremely weak and low,
He said, 'You must be joking –
Whatever could she know?'

Helena though stayed very calm,
She stood there quite serene;
Then quietly she told the king
Just who her dad had been.

This really made him listen,
For Narbon was *the* man.
He thought, 'If anything can cure,
I'm sure *his* potions can.'

But still he was reluctant,
So Narbon's daughter said,
'If you're not better in two days
I'll sacrifice my head.'

So finally the king agreed
But said, 'Let me be plain:
If you don't bring about a cure,
If I'm not right as rain...

'Within the passing of two days,
Well then it's sad to say,
You'll lose your life immediately,
Upon that very day.

'But if it works, then as reward
For taking such a chance,
I'll give you any man you want
From all the men in France.

'And then you shall be married to
The husband of your choice.'
So spoke the sick and ailing king
In weak and trembling voice.

~ ~ ~

The trust that Helena reposed
Upon her father's skills
Was happily well-founded for
His potions and his pills...

Were just the thing – they did the trick;
The king sat up in bed.
'I feel as if I'm good as new –
Completely cured,' he said.

The king was faithful to his word;
He gathered all the court.
He said, 'Choose any man you want,
It's what your skill has bought.'

Helena looked around the room
And saw him standing there –
The man she loved, dear Bertram –
And with a silent prayer...

She said, 'This is the man I want;
This is the one, my lord.'
But sadly Bertram didn't feel
Of similar accord.

He made it very clear to all.
He said, 'My gracious sir,
She is a common maiden and
I do not fancy her.

'She's servant to my mother,
She's frightfully lowborn.'
Poor Helena was shocked to hear
These words of total scorn.

But noblemen do not refuse
A gift from royalty.
The king said, 'Don't you dare reject
A gift that's come from me.'

And so upon that very day
The two of them were wed.
But it was not a happy time,
For it must now be said...

That though kings issue high decrees
From on their throne above,
The greatest monarch cannot grant
The gift of man's true love.

As soon as they were married
Bertram told his wife,
'I am not staying here at court,
I'm off to get a life.

'You must return to mother.'
And Helena – so good –
Just bowed her head in servitude
And meekly said she would.

When she got back the countess was
As nice as she could be.
She said, 'That selfish boy of mine
Will be the death of me.

'How can he send you back like this
And on your wedding day?
It really doesn't do at all –
I don't know what to say.'

But then things went from bad to worse.
A servant brought a note
From Helena's new husband,
And this is what he wrote:

'My wife I write to tell you that
You'll not see me again.
However long you wait around,
Your wait will be in vain.

'I'll only be your husband
If you contrive to take
The ring that's on my finger –
But wife, make no mistake...

'This ring stays on my finger, so
I think you should ensure
You don't waste time in thinking of
This husband anymore.

'But if you can obtain the ring,
Though stuck to me like glue,
Then I'll consider being
A loyal spouse to you.'

And then he wrote, 'One final thing
That I must stipulate,
You must be pregnant with our child
For me to be your mate.

'Then and only then will I
Stay faithful, loyal, true,
And be a selfless, loving, kind,
Husband unto you.'

Helena read the hurtful words,
Her eyes glazed in a trance,
For Bertram then went on to write,
That he was leaving France.

'Oh what a naughty, selfish boy!'
The countess cried aloud.
'You deserve a better man,
Not one that's rude and proud.'

She did the best she could to make
The sad, young girl feel better,
But her new daughter was destroyed
By this cruel, callous letter.

~ ~ ~

Next day the young wife ran away,
Nowhere could she be found,
They couldn't find her anywhere
Although they looked around.

And then they saw a solemn note
Inscribed in her fair hand:
'I've gone as pilgrim to the shrine
Of good Saint Jaques le Grand.

'I've gone to seek atonement
For driving him away,
I've gone to seek forgiveness,
I've gone there now to pray.

'Tell Bertram that I fled from here,
And though my love will burn,
Tell him that his detested wife
Will never now return.'

~ ~ ~

Bertram had gone to Florence,
And joined the army there,
But then he heard that his new wife
Had disappeared somewhere.

The countess wrote to tell him that
There was no need to roam,
As Helena had gone away –
So he could now come home.

Just when he was preparing
To go and see his mum,
Helena, quite unaware
Had made her plans to come...

To Florence – as a pilgrim;
She journeyed to the shrine,
And she was searching for a place
To stay awhile and dine.

She found lodgings with a widow,
And what a lucky find,
For the lady gave warm welcome,
And was extremely kind.

Once Helena had settled in
She said, 'I thought you might
Be pleased to view the army,
It's really quite a sight.

'They've just come back from fighting
In the recent wars,
And if you come along, you'll see
A countryman of yours.

'It is the Count of Roussillon,
He'll be there in the show.'
This was all it took to get
Young Helena to go.

For she would now see Bertram.
They headed for the place,
And on arriving she was pleased
To see his handsome face.

The widow was excited,
She said, 'Is he not fine?
He is so rich and handsome
And is of noble line.'

Helena, of course, agreed,
But then the widow said,
'Although he has a wife they say
He married her then fled.

'He rushed to leave his lady;
He joined the army here,
But now he's found another girl
And holds her very dear.

'He's fallen for my daughter –
Diana is her name –
And wooing her throughout the night
Is now his devious game.

'He sits beneath her window
Almost every night.
He sings her songs and praises her
While she keeps out of sight.

'He makes her propositions;
He does his very best
To come into her chamber while
The household's all at rest.

'Of course, my daughter won't agree.
She never would be caught
Behaving in a naughty way,
For she's a decent sort.'

What dreadful news for Helena:
That Bertram was untrue –
But with a flash of cleverness
She saw just what to do.

Apparently her Bertram
Had told the girl that day
That on the following morning
He would be on his way.

He'd begged Diana to allow,
(Although it wasn't right)
For him to come to her, just once
Upon that very night.

Helena told the widow then,
'Madam, you should know
That Bertram is my husband,
And I still love him so.

'Even though he hates me
I want to do one thing,
And that is to obtain from him
A beautiful gold ring.

'Now if your daughter would agree
To meet with Bertram later,
And once she has arranged all this,
Well then – to play a traitor.

'If she would let me take her place,
My husband would believe
He's meeting with your daughter,
And thus I could retrieve...

'The ring he promised, if I owned,
Would then ensure I gained
My Bertram's love for evermore,'
She quietly explained.

(You will recall that Bertram
Had promised his sad wife,
'Get me to give this ring to you
And I'll be yours for life.')

The widow and her daughter said,
'We will do all we can
To help you turn your husband
Into a faithful man.'

So Helena then set about
The first part of her scheme,
By sending information out
To Bertram that would seem...

To indicate his wife was dead,
(She did not care she lied)
For this would cause him to propose
Diana for his bride.

But it would be his Helena
Dressed up in a disguise;
He wouldn't know his worthy wife
Stood there before his eyes.

~ ~ ~

And so young Bertram came that night,
And with a lover's charm,
Did everything a young man could
To totally disarm...

While Helena took pains to play
A beauty with fine grace,
And Bertram didn't recognise
His spouse's lovely face.

He asked her hand in marriage,
And still he didn't guess,
Not even when she boldly gave
The longed for answer – 'Yes!'

Finally she said to him,
'Will you give me one thing
To bind our loving union here –
Please may I have your ring?'

He gave it in a moment
And said, 'It's yours for life –
A token of the faithful love
I'll give you as my wife.'

And Helena then handed him
A lovely silver ring,
A very special gift that had
Been given by the king.

Then just before the daylight broke
Young Bertram went away;
He didn't really want to leave –
In fact, he begged to stay.

But finally he left her there.
The unsuspecting chap
Had no idea that he'd been caught
Within a honey trap.

~ ~ ~

Bertram left to see his mum,
And once well on his way,
Helena to the widow said,
'Please come with me, I pray...

'To Paris – we must leave at once –
And bring Diana too,
For we must go to see the king
As there is much to do.'

But when they reached the palace,
The king had gone away.
He'd left to see the countess –
To make a little stay.

~ ~ ~

When the king beheld the countess,
He with compassion said,
'I am extremely sorry
That Helena is dead.'

Everyone was quite convinced
That Helena had died.
This was, of course, as we well know
Because the girl had lied.

Now Lord Lafeu was there, he said,
'I've thought it all along,
That Bertram caused a great offence –
He did an awful wrong.'

The king had listened carefully,
Then spoke, 'You know, I fear,
To yearn for those who have now died
May keep their memory dear...

'But we should let them rest in peace
Now sadly they are dead,
And to the living show our love,'
He solemnly then said.

'So I'll forgive young Bertram –
Summon him right now.'
Thus Bertram came before the king
And gave a sweeping bow.

He said, 'I'm truly sorry
For everything I've done.'
The king said he'd forgive him,
'Because you are the son...

'Of my old friend, your father,
And of the countess here,
And for the sake of Helena
Who's gone from us I fear.'

The king then gave his pardon.
He said he would restore
The young man to his favour
And call him 'friend' once more.

But almost as the words came out
His face creased in a frown:
The silver ring of Helena
He saw on looking down.

It was on Bertram's finger.
How had he got the ring?
For this had been a gift to her
From himself - the king.

It looked distinctly dubious.
The king said, 'Tell me sir,
That silver ring is Helena's –
Did you steal it from her?'

Bertram was truly flummoxed –
He huffed and puffed and sighed.
And then he looked straight at the king
And boldly then he lied.

He said, 'A woman threw this from
A window up above;
It was a silly gesture
Of hero worship love.'

But the king was well aware
That Bertram loathed his wife,
And felt that it looked likely
He'd taken her sweet life.

'Seize him' the king commanded.
Bertram shook in great alarm
For then a burly soldier
Grabbed him by the arm.

But then the widow entered;
She came onto the scene.
The king asked rather angrily,
'Whatever does this mean?'

Diana then came in and she
Addressed the crowded room.
She asked the king to there and then,
Make Bertram be her groom.

She said that this rogue, Bertram
Had said he'd marry her.
Bertram looking very flushed
Said, 'This is untrue, sir.'

He lied because he feared the king
Would vent more wrath on him;
That he'd be angry for what seemed
A young man's fickle whim.

Diana showed them all a ring –
She said, 'You gave me this,
And promised that you'd marry me
And sealed it with a kiss.'

It was the ring he'd given
To Helena that night,
Which she had passed to Diana –
But now they got a fright...

Because the king said, 'Seize her!
Hold Bertram and this maid.
I think the pair are murderers –
I'm very much afraid...

'That they have killed dear Helena,
And if I find it's so,
Then to the executioner
The pair of them will go.'

The king took this quick action
Because he was confused,
Their stories seemed to indicate
That somehow they'd ill-used...

Young Helena – and thus it was
His mind was filled with doubt;
They'd be his captives till he found
What this was all about.

Diana now was petrified
But then she begged the king,
'Please let my mother fetch the one
From whom we gained this ring.'

The widow went and then came back,
And to their great surprise
There stood the lovely Helena,
Alive before their eyes.

The countess was quite overjoyed,
She cried, 'My dear, it's you.'
The king with great amazement said,
'Can all these things be true?

'Is this young Bertram's ill-used wife?'
She answered, 'To my shame,
I'm but a shadow of a spouse,
A wife, in only name.'

Then turning to her husband, she
Declared, 'I now must say
It was your wife with whom you slept
On that romantic day.

'But I am sure you will recall,
That you were of a mind
To be extremely amorous,
And also very kind.

'You gave me this love token, which
Is such a lovely thing.'
She took it from Diana then
And handed him the ring.

'You gave me this, dear Bertram,
And you'll recall you said
The day I made this bauble mine,
We'd be completely wed.

'And I must tell you honestly,
(She thought, "Will he be riled?")
That now, I'm sure, I'm carrying
Our own dear precious child.

'So I command you faithfully,
Do what you said you'd do:
Become a loving husband now,
Be steady, upright, true.'

Bertram replied, 'With all my heart,
And I will prove to be
Most faithful and most loving –
Rely on it, you'll see.'

What an amazing turnaround –
The strangest ever heard!
And Bertram from that day was true
And loyal to his word.

The king said to Diana then,
'You've helped this lady, so
We'll find a worthy husband
For you, before you go.'

What it is to be a king –
Whatever can one say?
It is a king's prerogative
To match-make in this way.

So everything was sorted out.
There's nothing more to tell;
And happily it's true to say
All's well, that ended well!

He dressed up as a friar

MEASURE FOR MEASURE

Laws are there to be obeyed –
I think that's fair enough.
But sometimes folk will take no heed
Of all that legal stuff.

Thus it was in old Vienna,
For here they had a law
That all the city's residents
Chose simply to ignore.

It stated that you couldn't live
With someone not your wife;
And if this law was broken
You stood to lose your life.

But the duke who should enforce
The laws the State had made,
Took very little trouble
To see they were obeyed.

So every day he'd get complaints
By parents who were mad
Because their daughters chose to live
With men they viewed as bad.

Marriage grew uncommon –
A sad state of affairs,
No wonder parents were stressed out
With all their many cares.

The duke saw something must be done
But he was scared to act
Because the people loved him –
He knew this for a fact.

So if he changed completely,
And now enforced the law,
He feared his subjects would then cease
To love him anymore.

So he decided that he'd leave
Vienna for a while,
Putting someone else in charge
Who had a different style.

Then the law could be applied,
And he'd not get the blame.
He chose a friend to take the helm,
One Angelo by name.

Now Angelo was one all thought
Had led a blameless life;
He was the man to make quite sure
The young men took a wife.

His reputation spotless,
He really was a saint,
He was the man without a doubt
To sort out a complaint.

Even the duke's chief counsellor,
Lord Escalus by name,
Declared at once that Angelo
Would stop the young folk's game.

'I'm off to Poland,' said the duke –
But didn't really go;
He dressed up as a friar, thus
Nobody there would know...

That he was in Vienna still.
His reason was, you see,
To keep an eye on Angelo,
To find out if he'd be...

A better man at running things.
'Will Angelo,' he thought,
'Handle things efficiently
Once I have left the court?'

~ ~ ~

Now just when Angelo took charge
A man called Claudio
Seduced a fair young lady –
He claimed he loved her so.

And he had set up home with her;
He cared for her a lot,
But had he made her his dear wife?
The truth was – he had not.

Said Angelo immediately,
'Since this has now arisen
I know the course we must pursue:
Fling Claudio into prison.

'And he must pay the penalty
For this great wrong,' he said,
'And so I sentence him to lose
His most unworthy head.'

Lord Escalus was very shocked
And tried to intervene.
He said, 'Beheading Claudio
Will seem extremely mean.

'Besides his dad's a decent chap;
For his sake, please forgive.
For mercy's sake show some restraint
And let the young man live.'

But Angelo would not be moved.
He said, 'One thing's for sure —
If we release him, then we make
A scarecrow of the law.

'We set the law to frighten
All gloating birds of prey,
But then we let them perch on it
And don't chase them away.

'So it becomes a comfy perch,
And causes no-one terror;
Now if we let this happen
'Twill be a major error.

'This is my way of thinking,
And thus my reason why,
The prisoner can't be released
And why he has to die.'

Claudio's old friend, Lucio,
Then went to him in jail;
He said, 'You're in big trouble –
They won't allow you bail.

'In fact, the word out on the street
Is that you're dead for sure.
Angelo has made it clear
He will uphold the law.

'The duke would have excused you,'
Good Lucio quietly said,
'But this self-righteous idiot
Simply wants you dead.'

Claudio said, 'I've got one hope:
Go to my sister, pray.
She enters Saint Clare's nunnery
To take the veil today.

'Go tell dear Isabella
About the mess I'm in.
Tell her she is my only hope –
She is my closest kin.

'Ask her to go to Angelo
And beg him pardon me;
I'm sure her fluent discourse and
Her prayers can make him see

'That I do not deserve to die.
Tell her to beg the lord
To grant me a reprieve – and say
He's going overboard.'

~ ~ ~

Isabella – at the convent,
Was speaking with a nun,
Learning all the many rules
Of what she'd now begun...

When suddenly they heard a shout.
The nun said, 'Go and see
What that noise is all about
And then come back to me...

'For I can't speak to any man,
I can't return his hail;
It is forbidden totally
Once you're beneath the veil.

'And hark! – I hear him call again.
Please go to him, I pray,
And ask him why he breaks the peace
Of convent life today?'

Isabella left the nun.
She went to Lucio,
And said, 'What are you yelling for?
The nuns all want to know.'

Then Lucio said, 'Fair virgin, maid –
For so you seem to be –
I've come to seek a novice,
To give some help to me.

'Her name is Isabella,
It's crucial that I find
This lady who I'm told is both,
Compassionate and kind.

'Unhappy Claudio sent me –
He's in a sorry state.
Only his loving sister
Can save him from his fate.'

'*Unhappy* – why?' she asked him.
'I am the one you seek.
What's happened to my brother since
I spoke to him last week?'

Lucio said, 'He's been locked up;
He has seduced a maid,
And sends me here to ask if you
Will come now to his aid.'

'It's Juliet,' she softly said.
'She is a friend of mine.
But surely if he marries her
Then all will be just fine.'

Lucio replied, 'Of course,
That would be common sense.
But Angelo insists he die
Just for this small offence.

'Why, Claudio would marry her
At once – for this I know –
But Angelo will not agree
And lets his hatred grow.

'So Claudio's fervent hope is that
You will now go and see
This Angelo – and with your prayers
You'll set your brother free.'

Said Isabella, 'Angelo,
Will pay no heed to me;
Why in the world would he give ear
To my unworthy plea?'

Said Lucio, 'There is a chance –
When maidens weep and kneel
It really is amazing
What tears can make men feel.

'It makes them feel important –
Each stupid, useless clod
Believes he's something special
And thinks that he's a god.

'So go to wretched Angelo
And do the best you can,
And though he acts as if he's God,
Remember he's a man.'

~ ~ ~

So Isabella fled to court
And said to Angelo,
'I am a humble sister
Borne down with grief and woe.'

He answered her in haughty tones,
(In truth he thought her cute)
'So tell me then, young lady,
The nature of your suit?'

She pleaded for her brother's life
In the most moving way.
Angelo listened patiently
To all she had to say.

When she had finished he declared
By way of a reply,
'I cannot save your brother,
I'm sorry – he must die.

'He's broken our Vienna's law
And so it has to be;
To lose his life, I'm sad to say
Is now the penalty.'

She knelt to him for mercy –
He gave it to her straight:
'No power on Earth can save him,
He's sentenced – it's too late.'

She cried, 'If my poor brother
Were not himself, but you,
I feel I know for certain
Exactly what he'd do.

'A sister's plea would move him,
He wouldn't be so stern,
And this unhappy sentence,
I know he'd overturn.'

'You must accept,' said Angelo,
'What he's now got in store.
It is the proper sentence:
It is Vienna's law.

'Were he my dearest kinsman,
My brother or my son,
The law would have to run its course
For this base deed he's done.

'And for this reason, I'm afraid
Your brother dies tomorrow.'
'Oh spare him,' Isabella cried,
Borne down with dreadful sorrow.

'No-one else has paid this price
For doing what he's done.
And if you sentence him to death,
He'll be the only one.

'Knock on the doorway of your heart
And ask the reason why
You think it so imperative
That my dear brother die?'

She looked at him with big brown eyes,
Her face was drawn and ashen;
Her beauty made him start to feel
An overpowering passion.

His mind was now in conflict –
He wondered what to do.
Then Isabella pleaded,
'Can bribes amend your view?'

'What's that you say?' he sternly asked.
'How could you even dare?'
'Oh, not with treasure, lord,' she said,
'But with a fervent prayer.'

'Come tomorrow,' he replied,
'I'll hear no more today.'
She left him grateful that she'd gained
A day's reprieve this way.

~ ~ ~

Once she had gone, sly Angelo
Reflected very much.
'Perhaps I am in love,' he thought.
'I hunger for her touch.

'I've never felt this way before –
I've always been above
Such feelings – for I've always laughed
When others are in love.'

That night he could not sleep at all;
Her image filled his head.
I think we all can guess just where
His naughty thoughts now led.

He struggled to resist them,
But he was doomed to fail;
He'd tell her of a way to get
Her brother out of jail.

Yes – he who'd hardly listened to
Her desperate diatribe
In which she'd offered openly
Her pious, prayerful bribe...

Would turn to his advantage now
Her current state of strife:
He would seduce her in exchange
For her dear brother's life.

~ ~ ~

So when she came next morning –
He said, 'Just yield to me,
Give up your virgin honour
And I'll set Claudio free.

'I adore you, Isabella;
My feelings are sincere.'
She said, 'That's how my brother felt;
He held his Juliet dear.

'And for his ardour he's to die –
Surely that's not right.'
'Oh he shall live, if you,' he said,
'Will come to me tonight.'

The saintly girl was horrified
That he proposed this pact;
The same crime as her brother –
It was the selfsame act.

'Is this to test my virtue?'
She said in great dismay.
'This *has* to be the reason
You speak to me this way.'

He replied, 'It is no test,
I mean just what I speak.
For by this pact we each can gain
The object that we seek.'

Isabella raged against
All that he had unfurled.
She cried with great emotion,
'I'll tell the whole wide world...

'Just what kind of man you are.'
He said, 'You try that game,
And no-one will believe you;
Remember my good name.

'I'm well-known for my pious ways,
So do not waste your time.
Do what I want or Claudio
Will perish for his crime.

'Take care before you answer,
Come along tomorrow;
Agree to my suggestion and
We'll put an end to sorrow.'

~ ~ ~

Isabella left the court
Feeling much maligned;
She went to see her brother in
The place he was confined.

Arriving at the jail she ran
Straight to her brother's cell;
She found a pious, friendly friar
Was visiting as well.

This was, in fact, the noble duke
Whom no-one recognised,
For he was cleverly attired –
Quite artfully disguised.

He'd spoken to fair Juliet,
Depressed by what she'd done;
She'd claimed, 'It isn't Claudio's fault,
For I'm the guilty one.'

And then he'd come to Claudio
Who also was contrite.
The duke was much encouraged for
They'd both learnt wrong from right.

When Isabella entered
She gave Claudio a kiss.
The startled friar looked up and said,
'Who in the world is this?'

She said, 'I've come to speak a word
With my poor brother there.
Please leave us on our own awhile;
He'll profit from my care.'

The gentle friar left the cell
But he was keen to hear
The talk that passed between them,
So stood outside, quite near.

He heard young Claudio enquire,
Once he had closed the door,
'Tell me, good sister – what's the news?
Please tell me, what's the score?'

Isabella tried to be
Composed, and took a breath,
Then said, 'Dear brother, I'm afraid
You must prepare for death.'

'Oh, is there nothing can be done?
Is there no hope?' he said.
'You must accept,' she answered him,
'That you're as good as dead.

'For though there is a certain way
That I could rescue you,
I'd have to carry out an act
You'd not want me to do.

'For Angelo has promised,
If I sleep with him,' she said,
'He'll spare you – but the price I pay
Is I must share his bed.

'I would gladly give my life
To save you, brother dear,
But thus to lose my virtue
Would be too much I fear.'

Claudio listened silently,
Then with a desperate cry
He said, 'Sweet sister, save me,
For I don't want to die.

'The deed that Angelo demands
Is not so much to give,
For it is one that will ensure
I have a chance to live.

'Nature will forgive you,
For I have heard folk say
A sin becomes a virtue when
Committed in this way.

'Let me live dear sister,
For you are now empowered
To save me – and it only means
That you will be deflowered.'

She called him 'Faithless coward! Wretch!'
Said she despised his name
For wanting to preserve his life
By his poor sister's shame.

'If you had twenty heads to lose
On twenty blocks,' she said,
'They should be used to save me from
This Angelo's foul bed.'

'Hear me out,' then Claudio cried;
Before he could say more
The duke appeared in friar's garb
And peered around the door.

He said, 'I have heard everything,
And say to both of you
That Angelo is not corrupt –
I can't believe it's true.

'It's a test for Isabella.
Why he performs this act.
He'll be relieved when he finds out
Your honour stays intact;

'So pleased that you denied him,
You passed his little test.
Don't fret about it anymore –
It's not a real request.

'But as for you, young Claudio,
There is no hope I fear,
All you can do is pray because
I feel your death draws near.'

Claudio then repented –
Ashamed for being weak;
He turned to face his sister,
'Please listen while I speak.

'Forgive me for my weakness,
Please try to pardon me;
I am so tired of life that death
Can come and set me free.'

Claudio was quite overwhelmed;
His sister then forgave –
She knew it was the fear of death
That made him act the knave.

She left then with the friar, who said,
'The hand that made you fair
Was also one that made you good,
Of this I'm now aware.'

'Oh dear!' she cried. 'If when he left
The duke could have conceived
What Angelo would prove to be –
How he would be deceived...

'He'd not have left Vienna in
Such untrue hands as these;
He'd not have let this Angelo
Become a foul disease.

'And if some day the duke returns
I'll tell him all I know;
I'll tell him of my brother's death
And of vile Angelo.'

Little did she know that as
She made this stern rebuke,
The man to whom she now addressed
Her comments was the duke.

The 'friar' replied that Angelo
Would say she told a lie,
Then said, 'I think I can make sure
That Claudio doesn't die.

'If you will do all that I say,
If you will just be strong,
I think that I can show a way
To right this dreadful wrong.'

Isabella said that she
Would trust the holy friar,
For after all a man of God
Would scarcely be a liar.

The friar then told her of his plan.
He asked, 'Now have you heard
Of Mariana, lone and sweet,
And what to her occurred?'

'I've heard about this lady,'
The anxious girl replied.
'Well, sad to say,' the friar said,
'Her dearest brother died.

'This Mariana was betrothed
To awful Angelo.'
'He was to wed!' she cried aghast.
'Well, that I didn't know.'

'Oh yes, but now he does disown
His intended wife.
Her brother was at sea when thus
He sadly lost his life.

'He had his sister's dowry
To give to Angelo,
The ship went down and it was lost –
A really bitter blow.

'Then Angelo, that selfish cur
Disowned his would be spouse;
He made up tales about her
And banned her from his house.

'I found this out just recently –
So this is what we'll do;
Tell Angelo that you agree
To what he's asked of you.

'Say you will go at midnight,
And he must free your brother.
But my dear, you will not go,
For we will send another.

'Mariana will be sent.
There is no sin in this,
For they're as good as married,
So nought can be amiss.

'Mariana will agree
For I have been to her,
To give her consolation –
I know that she'll concur.'

~ ~ ~

So returning then to Angelo,
Isabella said, 'All right!
I'll do the very thing you ask
And come to you tonight.'

'And in return,' he then replied,
'I'll pardon Claudio.
So we have reached agreement –
But this you need to know…

'This key will gain admittance to
My palace here tonight.
Enter by the vineyard gate
And keep well out of sight.'

So they agreed the meeting;
She left without a word,
Then went to meet the friar
To tell what had occurred.

He was at Mariana's.
She, delighted with the plan,
Was quite convinced it would unite
Her once more with her man.

Her face all veiled in shadows –
And hidden from his sight –
Sly Angelo would never know
Who was his love that night.

So Mariana made her way
To see him as arranged,
Disguised as Isabella –
Their roles had been exchanged.

Once she had gone to Angelo
The duke, still dressed as friar,
Went to the prison for he thought
Angelo a liar.

And it was very lucky that
He did so choose to go,
For word had just arrived, right then,
From evil Angelo.

The order was the very thing
That Isabella dreaded.
It said that Claudio that night
Must swiftly be beheaded.

The document went on to say
That Claudio's severed head
Be brought to Angelo forthwith,
While he was still abed.

What a devious, evil man
So full of bile and hate.
The duke on hearing this made haste
To check on Claudio's fate.

Claudio was still alive –
The duke then made his way
To see the Provost there in charge,
Where he had this to say:

'Here is a letter from the duke –
See there, his noble seal.'
The Provost looked to ascertain
That this device was real.

The letter gave strict orders
To spare poor Claudio.
The Provost said, 'What in the world
Can I tell Angelo?

'He'll want some proof of Claudio's death...
He'll want his severed head,
And it will be the worse for me
If I refuse,' he said.

But after some discussion
They hit upon a plan:
They'd send a different head to him,
That of another man.

A prisoner'd been beheaded
Earlier that day.
They'd send *his* head to Angelo
And fool him in this way.

For Claudio and this dead man
Each looked like the other,
So Angelo would think the head
Was Isabella's brother.

The head was sent that instant,
And then the good duke wrote
To Angelo – and this is what
He said in his brief note.

'I'm coming to Vienna.
Meet me at the city gate.
Tell everyone I'm coming.
Be there – and don't be late.

'And also tell my people that
If they require redress
From grave injustice, then ask me –
I'll sort out any mess.

'So let the news be spread abroad,
I want you to proclaim
That I, the duke, am coming back.'
He signed his proper name.

~ ~ ~

Next morning Isabella,
Quite early, made her way
To prison so that she could see
Young Claudio that day.

The friar, because he had a plan
Told her, 'Your brother's dead,
Angelo had him killed last night –
Cut off his head,' he said.

'The head's been sent to Angelo.'
The friar held nothing back,
And suddenly the world she knew
Was turned completely black.

'Unhappy Claudio!' she cried.
'Oh wicked Angelo!
How could he tell me all those lies?
How could he stoop so low?'

The friar tried to calm her down,
But then he left her there.
He went away and laid aside
His friar's garb with care.

And he made ready to address
His people on that day,
In just the way he'd always done
Before he went away.

Then as the duke he reappeared,
Acclaimed by high and low –
And waiting for him at their head
Was wicked Angelo.

And as the duke passed through the crowd
Brave Isabella cried,
'My Lord, please hear my sorry suit
Of how my brother died.'

She told him everything she knew –
Though Angelo cried, 'Liar!'
'You'll know I speak the truth,' she said,
'When you have heard the friar.'

The duke then said, 'Now Angelo
And Escalus – hold trial,
To get the truth of all these things;
I'll leave you for a while.'

Angelo was very pleased
To judge in his own cause;
He could interpret how he liked
Vienna's ancient laws.

The duke was not away for long;
Just long enough to dress
In friar's clothes – then he returned
To sort out all the mess.

Lord Escalus then asked the friar,
'Did you excite things thus?
Did you, sir, slander Angelo?
And perpetrate this fuss?'

The 'friar' gazed back calmly
And said to this rebuke,
'I will not answer you, my lord.
I want to see the duke.'

Said Escalus, 'We'll hear you now.
Don't dare to make a fuss!
Speak out clearly, honestly –
The duke is here *in us*.'

The friar spoke out boldly.
'I blame the duke,' he said,
'For letting this man judge the maid
He tried to lure to bed.'

The friar carried on to say,
'Well, I have looked around,
And I must tell you truthfully
I don't like what I've found.

'The state is everywhere corrupt,
The duke has let things slip;
He should have stayed and not gone off
Upon his little trip.'

Escalus got really mad
To hear him speak this way.
'How dare you stand and criticise
The good duke here today?'

He threatened him with awful things,
And said, 'Take him to jail.
Incarcerate him for a while
And don't allow him bail.'

But then to his amazement
And everyone's surprise,
The duke stood tall so all could see
And threw off his disguise.

Angelo turned ashen-faced,
His heartbeat leapt in speed,
He guessed the duke was well aware
Of his disgraceful deed.

He knew his guilt was clear to see,
He'd lost his once good name.
'Sentence me to death,' he cried,
'And don't prolong my shame.'

'I trusted you,' the duke exclaimed.
'But you just ran amok.
You, wretch, shall die like Claudio
Upon the selfsame block.

'To you, fair Mariana
I would suggest a plan:
Go and search the whole wide world
And find another man.'

But Mariana up and said,
'I crave none else, my lord.'
She begged for Angelo's base life,
She went quite overboard.

'Oh Isabella, please,' she said,
'I beg for you to tell
The noble duke to spare his life –
For if you plead as well...

'He'll listen to you more than me,
I know this to be true.
Oh Isabella, please, oh please,
Oh, I implore you to.'

Without delay, the gracious girl
Dropped down upon her knees;
To those of Mariana –
She added her own pleas.

She said, 'He was an honest man
Until he looked at me;
For heaven's sake, show mercy
And set the sinner free.

'My brother was shown justice in
A twisted kind of way,
The thing for which he died –he did;
This fact I can't gainsay.'

The duke said, 'Well now, Angelo,
Make this sweet girl your wife,
For Mariana's pleadings
Have surely saved your life.'

Angelo felt great relief
Now he was in the clear,
He went to Mariana and
He gently called her 'Dear.'

The duke then summoned Claudio
And to his sister said,
'Here's your lamented brother – see
He is not really dead.'

Isabella was amazed.
The duke's kind face was set;
'Claudio,' he commanded,
'You must wed Juliet.'

He pardoned Claudio right there,
Then to his sister said –
'Give me your hand fair lady,
For we should now be wed.'

Isabella was in love –
She put aside the veil;
So there's a happy ending to
A nearly tragic tale:

And sweet Isabella –
Who was so fine and good –
Set such a great example
Throughout the neighbourhood...

That no girls lived unmarried with
Their boyfriends anymore:
They eagerly took husbands all –
And thus obeyed the law!

He awoke and gazed about

A MIDSUMMER NIGHT'S DREAM

Now maybe you've already heard,
You may already know,
How once in Athens city state,
So many years ago...

Fathers were allowed to choose
Just who their daughters wed,
And no surprise most daughters did
Just what their daddy said.

For in those far off, ancient times,
Those distant days of yore,
Great Athens was encumbered with
A really stringent law.

For if a father told his girl,
'You will now wed this guy.'
And she replied all sulkily,
'No dad – I'd rather die,'

The father then with careful thought
And after a deep breath,
Could have his daughter thrown in jail
Or even put to death.

So if a daughter was intent
On safely growing old,
The wisest course, without a doubt,
Was do as she was told.

Of course, it's very fair to say
Most fathers loved their daughters,
And so they couldn't contemplate
Such awful, bloody slaughters.

And thus this strange and ancient law
Was very seldom used,
And lovelorn girls who disobeyed
Were generally excused.

~ ~ ~

But then one sunny, summer's day
A lovely looking girl,
Fell in love and deeply too –
Her heart was in a whirl.

But her old dad, Egeus
On hearing this news said,
'You marry that unworthy youth
And I will see you dead.'

Sweet Hermia, the daughter, sighed,
For she was very sad.
She cried, 'I beg you think again.
I love Lysander dad.'

Egeus very clearly saw
His daughter's love was true,
But wouldn't change his mind and said,
'I've found the man for you.

'Demetrius is a decent lad
And he's the one you'll wed.'
She replied and forcefully,
'I'd rather I were dead!'

Egeus was annoyed and thus
Answered her rebuke;
'I'm having none of this from you.
We'll go and see the duke!'

She realised that Athen's duke
Would tell them what to do,
His word in Athens was the law,
As Hermia well knew.

And so she was concerned about
What might now be in store,
If the duke, quite literally
Applied the rule of law.

~ ~ ~

Now this great duke was known to be
Both reasonable and kind,
And of a fair and rational
And decent turn of mind.

His judgements were considered fair
By everyone he saw,
For they were strictly bound right to
The letter of the law.

Hermia now with nervousness
Looked at the good duke's face,
And slowly, then with confidence
She made her lovelorn case.

She said, 'I know Demetrius,
In many ways is fine,
But if I lived a hundred years
He never could be mine.

'For he once loved fair Helena
Who is my closest friend,
He vowed with passion that his love
For her would never end.

'But now in just a moment
He sets Helena free,
And strangely now he makes the claim
That he's in love with me.

'And though he says of Helena
He has now had his fill,
My dear, sweet friend declares that she
Loves her Demetrius still.

'There's nothing she can do to quell
This very strong attraction.
Demetrius now owns her heart.
She loves him to distraction.'

Although the duke was most intent
On being just and fair,
And though he felt great pity for
Hermia standing there...

He said, 'My best advice is this,
Agree ere it's too late,
For you must dutifully obey
The laws of our great state.

'So marry good Demetrius,'
The duke then firmly said,
'Or otherwise there is a chance
That you might end up dead.

'In four days time you must return
And come back here to me,
And if you've got good sense, my dear,
You'll say that you agree.'

Poor Hermia gasped desperately
And she began to cry –
For though she'd not wed who they wished,
She didn't want to die.

The duke looked kindly on her, then
Dismissed her with a plea;
'I beg you to obey,' he said,
'Just marry him, for me.'

But Hermia was known to have
Extremely stubborn ways,
And though she knew she only had
The few forthcoming days...

To marry young Demetrius
Or face the fact she'd die,
She still loved her Lysander.
She was loyal to her guy.

~ ~ ~

When later on Lysander heard
Of her intended fate,
He told her not to worry
Or get into a state.

He said, 'My darling Hermia,
I know just what to do.
I know how we can sort this out –
How I can rescue you.

'I have a kindly, ancient aunt
Who lives some way from here,
And if I take you to her,
You can be free of fear.

'For only here in Athens
Is there a risk you'll die.
In many other places
This law does not apply.'

Lysander smiled with confidence
And then went on to say,
'Tonight when it gets very dark,
We must both steal away.

'Once your family are abed,
Creep softly from your house.
Make sure you do it carefully –
Be quiet as a mouse.

'Then rendezvous with me, my love
Within the nearby wood.'
And then he told her once again
So that she understood.

Thus with a clear agreement
The nervous lovers parted,
Though, in truth, young Hermia
No longer felt downhearted.

For now she sought out Helena,
Upon that very night,
And told her in great detail
About her sorry plight.

Helena was an honest girl
And her best friend, you see,
And so she told her everything
About their plan to flee.

She said, 'And once we're far away,
Well then we will get wed.'
'Congratulations to you both,'
Sweet Helena then said.

That is all she said and yet
She had her private views,
About sweet Hermia's sad plight
And of this breaking news.

Was she filled with jealousy
Or maybe being mean?
Or maybe just mischievous –
It's very hard to glean...

But she set off immediately,
In fact she quickly ran,
To tell her former lover –
Demetrius – the plan.

The fervent love she had for him
Still drove her quite insane,
But telling him about the plan –
What could she hope to gain?

No doubt he'd follow Hermia –
This she most surely knew;
It's what his love most certainly
Would make him want to do.

And her love for Demetrius
Which she could never quell,
Would make her go where e'er he went.
She'd follow him as well!

~ ~ ~

The tangled, eerie wood wherein
The lovers planned to meet,
Was trodden lightly every day
By lots of tiny feet...

Owned by the dainty people
That we have come to call
The fairies, and the reason is,
Because they're very small.

One, by the name of Oberon
Was the fairy king;
He told the others what to do.
Took charge of everything.

And all the fairies, young and old
Clearly understood,
The big boss was King Oberon
And he ruled all the wood.

At one time in the past, the king
Was often to be seen
With lovely, fair Titania,
His sweet and loyal queen.

And they would laugh and frolic
And join the fairy fun,
But now when it was time for play
The royal pair had none.

For every single time they met
Upon a summer's night,
Somewhere deep within the wood,
Bathed by the soft moonlight...

They'd look each other up and down
And it would not be long,
Before one of them said some words
That clearly were quite wrong.

And then they'd argue vehemently,
Just like little devils ,
And in a tick they would destroy
The joyful, midnight revels.

The fairies, every one of them
Would quickly run and hide,
And keep well hidden in the hope
The quarrel would subside.

Whatever was the reason
For this lack of joy?
Well simply put, 'twas all about
A little orphaned boy.

His mother who was now deceased
Had been Titania's friend,
But sadly giving birth had brought
This girl's life to an end.

And once she had been driven off
Within a sombre hearse,
The queen had gone to fetch the child
From his attentive nurse.

'I'll be your mummy now, sweet boy,'
All lovingly she'd said.
'So you don't need to worry that
Your own mama is dead.'

The boy had settled in, and well,
And was now of the age
To do some work – the king believed
He'd make a first-class page.

Thus Oberon was firmly set
And yes, extremely keen
To prise the little lad away
From his own fairy queen.

Titania though had other plans.
She'd not give up the boy,
Even though King Oberon
Tried every kind of ploy.

So this explains quite easily
Why every single night,
The king and queen, when e'er they met,
Would get into a fight.

~ ~ ~

Then one starry, moonlit eve
King Oberon was walking,
Surrounded by his splendid court
And they were idly talking…

When out of nowhere there appeared
Queen Titania's train;
They stopped and eyed each other
Upon that woodland lane.

And by a strange coincidence
This was the very night
That our two lovers planned to make
Their hasty desperate flight.

And shortly they were due to meet
Right in the selfsame wood
Wherein King Oberon and his queen
Angrily now stood.

'Well, fancy meeting you, my dear,'
Exclaimed the pompous king.
'This really is without a doubt
A most unpleasant thing!

'But as you're here before me now
I'll ask you once again,
And let me make my wishes clear;
I will be very plain.

'Obey me now and let me have
That little orphaned boy.'
The queen replied, 'I'll not agree
For he is not a toy.'

The king's face turned deep scarlet.
He flew into a rage.
'It's not a plaything that I want.
I simply want a page!'

The queen's eyes flashed displeasure.
She let out an angry cry.
'Your fairy kingdom far and wide,
Could never ever buy...

'The little orphaned boy – I vow
No matter what you say.'
Then Queen Titania turned her back
And hurried on her way.

'Go then,' the king cried out with bile.
'But this day you will rue,
For I will never let this lie.
I'll be revenged on you!

'And 'twill be done and long before
The morning clock has struck!'
And then in loud and raucous voice
He called his servant Puck.

Now Puck, this servant was most shrewd,
And keen and sharp and smart,
And he'd made having fun into
A devilish kind of art.

'Now, good Puck, be on your way,'
Said Oberon with glee,
'And bring the purple petals of
That special flower to me.

'We'll make some magic lover's juice
And then we'll softly creep
Up to my irksome queen, and while
She lies there fast asleep.

'And then we'll place some of the juice
Upon her eyelids, though –
We must use the lightest touch
So she will never know.

'And when she wakes from her deep sleep,
The first one whom she sees
Will make her heart beat very fast,
Bring tremors to her knees,

'And she will vow with passion
To the heavens above
That she is now besotted and
Quite passionately in love.'

Oh how young Puck loved all of this.
The mischief and the fun.
He couldn't wait to do his task
So went off at a run.

He said, 'This will be wonderful.
I'll go and get the flower.
And I'll be back beloved king,
Well within the hour.'

~ ~ ~

The king sat waiting patiently
For artful Puck's return,
And then through tangled trees he was
Just able to discern...

The handsome young Demetrius,
Then fair Helena too,
And as she followed him she called,
'Demetrius – I love you.'

Demetrius was responding –
He kept on saying, 'Go!'
And it was clear to anyone
He didn't want to know.

When she drew close he turned to her
And gave the girl a shove.
She cried out in a broken voice,
'What happened to your love?'

Demetrius replied in haste,
'Helena – let me be.
Just go away – leave me alone
And please don't hassle me.'

Sad Helena was most distraught.
This was hard to swallow.
And yet she there and then resolved,
'I still intend to follow.'

And omnipresent Oberon,
The curious fairy king,
Because he was invisible
Heard every little thing.

And as he watched this sorry scene
And saw events unfurl,
He felt a massive sympathy
For the lovesick girl.

Of course he knew that very soon
He would have the power
To do amazing, crafty tricks
With the magic flower.

For in an instant he could send
Old Cupids straight, true dart
Towards Demetrius and pierce
That errant lover's heart.

~ ~ ~

When Puck returned the king exclaimed,
'Without a doubt, forsooth,
There walks o'er yonder in our wood
A most unpleasant youth.

'And with him is a lovely girl
Whose beating heart doth burn
With a true and noble love
The youth does not return.

'So find him Puck and wait awhile
Until he falls asleep,
And then with cunning and great stealth,
You quietly must creep...

'And drop some of the juice you've brought
Onto the young man's eyes.
But do be careful not to wake
The youth there in surprise.

'And also mind that you ensure
The lady is close by,
For when he wakes this girl must be
The first he does espy.

'Go now my Puck and see it's done.
As ever do your worst.
And make quite sure the young lad sees
That lovely lady first!'

Then King Oberon made his way
To where Titania slept.
He had some of the magic juice
Which he had carefully kept.

He placed some drops upon her eyes
And to himself he said,
'You'll love whomever first you see.'
Then rapidly he fled.

~ ~ ~

Meanwhile, with apprehension
And softly as she could
Hermia left her father's house
And headed for the wood.

She nervously but happily,
Whilst taking every care,
Made her way towards the glade
To find Lysander there.

When she arrived she felt worn out
But still she did her best
To carry on, until she sighed,
'My love – I must have rest.'

So after searching carefully
They found a mossy mound
And both of them most gratefully
Sank down onto the ground.

'Sleep softly now till morning,'
Lysander kindly said.
'This mossy mound will have to act
As if it were a bed.'

In but a trice the loving pair
Were both soundly sleeping,
And then it was mischievous Puck
Came quietly a-creeping...

And when he thus perceived them there
Upon the ground asleep,
He stopped, he sighed, he took the time
To have a little peep.

Then to himself he smugly said,
'I do believe in truth
This is the girl the king described,
And this too is the youth.'

And so he placed some drops of juice
Onto Lysander's eyes,
And as he did he listened to
The lover's sleepy sighs.

Now as we know the king had meant
The purple juice to be
For young Demetrius and thus
That's what we thought we'd see.

But to be fair to artful Puck
He shouldn't take the blame,
For surely it is true to say
Most youths all look the same.

So kindly, well-intentioned Puck
Had made a small mistake,
And this is just so easily done –
Bad luck for goodness sake.

So Puck ran off all gleefully
Although he'd got it wrong,
Just at the very moment that
Helena came along.

Demetrius could run quite fast
And so he'd drawn ahead;
He'd left Helena all alone;
In truth, he had just fled.

But now Helena had espied
Lysander lying here,
She felt relieved and gladly thought
She had no more to fear.

'Oh dear Lysander,' she cried out,
'Oh for mercy's sake,
If you're alive then speak to me.
Oh please, good sir, awake.'

She acted out of innocence –
No thought of causing harm –
And of course she didn't know
About King Oberon's charm.

Lysander woke up wearily
And rubbed his tired eyes,
For in his distant dreams he'd heard
Helena's fervent cries.

As he awoke his eyes met hers
And in the merest tick,
The magic, purple juice had worked
Its very clever trick.

For with no hesitation,
He cried, 'My sweetest dove,
It's you Helena – you alone –
That I most truly love.'

Helena was mortified.
She knew he was engaged,
So rightly she was angry
And really felt enraged.

With trembling voice she coldly said,
'Why do you speak this way?
Whatever in this muddled world
Would your sweet Hermia say?

'I do not understand at all
What this is all about.'
He responded tartly,
With a heartfelt shout...

'It's over now between us.
We're not lovers anymore;
In fact I freely tell you that
She's really quite a bore.'

Helena was astounded.
She said, 'Love's not a game.
Lysander – you are fickle!
You men are all the same!'

She spoke with utmost vigour
And with a touch of candour.
'I'm disappointed and I thought
Much more of you Lysander.'

She carried on remorselessly.
She had her tearful say,
And then she turned upon her heel
And quickly ran away.

Lysander, though he was surprised,
Followed Helena too,
For he was now intent to show
That his new love was true.

He left Hermia where she was,
Soundly fast asleep –
Despite the noisy argument
She hadn't made a peep.

When later on the girl awoke
She found herself alone;
She was alarmed and mystified
To be there on her own.

What in the world had happened?
Where could Lysander be?
She couldn't think what might have caused
Her precious love to flee.

Why had he gone and disappeared
Without a single word?
She really couldn't understand
Whatever had occurred.

So jumping up she set out then
As quickly as she could
To search for him both far and wide
Throughout the massive wood.

~ ~ ~

Meanwhile Demetrius, full of love
Was busy searching too,
He ran about, he scanned the wood
Everywhere – right through.

His fervent love for Hermia
Now spurred him on and on,
Crazily, he wondered where
Sweet Hermia had gone.

Then finally when he was lost
And wondering what to do,
He grew extremely sleepy
And then he dozed off too.

But as he slept there in the wood –
By a stroke of luck –
King Oberon came walking by
Accompanied by Puck.

Deep in conversation,
They walked on through the wood;
The king was saying earnestly,
'This really isn't good.'

He wore a solemn frown, for he
Had been informed by Puck,
How his ingenious, clever plan
Had sadly come unstuck.

How Puck had made a bad mistake,
Applied the love charm to
The wrong young man asleep that night.
Of course all this you knew.

But Oberon was set to have
His pleasure and his whim.
He said, 'To rectify this now,
We must put some on him.

'The gentle youth you placed it on
Was, silly Puck, quite wrong.
The youth we see is who I meant,
'Twas this one all along.'

So as Demetrius, eyes shut,
Lay gently sleeping there,
The king poured purple, magic juice
Upon him and with care.

He tenderly placed drops onto
Each sleeping, closed eyelid,
Then Oberon and cheeky Puck
Both left the scene and hid.

~ ~ ~

Right at the very moment that
The fairy pair withdrew
The fast asleep Demetrius
Suddenly came to.

As he awoke and looked around
Who should come on the scene
But Helena, she stood right where
The fairies had just been.

So at the very moment
Demetrius awoke
He saw before him Helena
And lovingly he spoke...

Of passion, love and all those things
To totally disarm,
For he was now beneath the spell
Of all the juices charm.

Helena was perplexed of course.
However could this be?
But as she had this puzzled thought
She was surprised to see...

Lysander striding manfully,
Coming into view,
And there was tearful Hermia
Following him too.

But then on seeing Helena
Lysander spoke of love,
He said he loved her desperately,
His passion way above...

That for any other girl
That he had ever known.
Helena was dumbfounded and
Was now completely thrown.

For as Lysander cried out loud,
'Helena, I love you.'
Demetrius was quick to cry,
'I also love you too.'

Helena was annoyed and said,
'Why do you act this way?
For it's a really horrible
And most unkind display.'

Poor Hermia was most amazed –
Really quite astonished.
'What is this silly game you play?'
The angry girl admonished.

'So tell me Helena, my friend –
Is any of this true?
This motley pair who once loved me
Now say that they love you.'

'It does seem that it is the case,'
Perplexed Helena said.
'They loved you once but now it seems
They both love me instead.'

The conversation now between
The girls grew sharp and terse,
And then things went from very bad
To really much, much worse.

Demetrius and Lysander
Had both withdrawn from sight,
The youths had now decided
That they would have a fight.

And as they did the pair both swore
Unto the heavens above
That they would give their very life
For sweet Helena's love.

Puck and Oberon standing by
Saw the young men go.
The king exclaimed, 'What should we do?
It's really hard to know.

'Puck, good servant, we must try
To put these matters right –
We've got to intervene somehow
And try to stop this fight.

'There's only one thing we can do.
Cloak the wood with fog.
Use your magic skills and make
The thickest, blackest smog.

'And in this cunning manner –
This oh, so devious way,
We will confuse these warring lads
And lead them both astray.

'And to perplex them even more,
We'll mime their cries,' he said.
'You can do it clever Puck.
Make them go where they're led.

'If one of them is made to hear
What he believes to be
His rival's voice there in the fog,
Then he will run to see.

'Lead them round and round the wood.
Confuse the pair until
They are completely vexed and tired
And starting to feel ill.

'Then wait until the two of them
Have fallen fast asleep,
And when their sleep is of a kind
That is extremely deep...

'Then creep upon them silently
In their makeshift bower,
And drop this special juice that's from
A different kind of flower...

'On Lysander lying there –
Onto his closed eyelids –
And that should sort this fighting out
Between these lovelorn kids.

'For when Lysander wakes he'll find
That he has no recall
Of the happenings of this night –
No memory at all.

'And he'll love Hermia in the way
He always did before,
His fervent love for Helena
Will fly right out the door.

'And Demetrius will again
Love Helena – and thus
This will put a rapid end
To this unseemly fuss.

'And then as fast as anything
I think we will discern
That their old burning passion
Will hastily return.

'It will rekindle readily,
Just like a tired fire,
And then each girl will have the youth
Whom each of them desire.

'So go and sort it out good Puck.
Make sure you do it well.
And please make certain that you do
Exactly as I tell.

'And then when they awaken
I guarantee 'twill seem
That what has passed on this fraught night
Was merely but a dream.'

~ ~ ~

When Puck had done all this, he then
Mischievously just crept
Into the cosy, woodland glade,
Where Queen Titania slept.

But then quite unexpectedly
A movement caught his eye,
It was a man just fidgeting
As he slept there close by.

He was a weaver and his name
Was Bottom, and that day,
Whilst out a-roaming in the wood
He'd gone and lost his way.

As Puck stood gazing quietly
At the sleeping man,
Within his mind he naughtily
Hatched a fiendish plan.

'He shall be the queen's new love,'
Mischievously he said.
And out of nowhere conjured up
A mock-up ass's head.

He chuckled to himself as then
He stroked it tenderly.
He thought, 'This really will turn out
To be a sight to see.'

He placed it over Bottom's head
And then leaned back and sighed.
'Oh, it fits perfectly,' he laughed.
'It's not too tall or wide.'

And he was right, for Bottom there
Whereon the head did sit,
Now wore an ass's head that was
A truly perfect fit.

And then, though Puck had taken pains
To not make any sound,
Daft Bottom in his ass's head
Started coming round.

He awoke and gazed about
Completely unaware
Of the transformation
That had happened there.

And as he took a look around
And surveyed the scene,
He very quickly saw close by
The sleeping fairy queen.

And at that very moment
Titania woke and said,
As she in fascination
Looked at the ass's head...

'Whoever is this handsome beau –
This lovely sight I see?
A holy angel from above
Most surely it must be.

'And are you also affable
And very wise as well?
Now speak up boldly handsome sir
And please, I pray, do tell.'

Bottom looked down at the queen
From in his ass's hood.
He said, 'The only thing I want
Is to escape this wood.'

'Oh, please don't speak of leaving,'
Cried the stricken queen.
The magic juice was working
And making her most keen...

To do whatever she could do
To get the ass to stay.
She pleaded desperately and cried,
'Oh, please don't go away.

'And don't play games or even think
Of trifling with me;
This is no common fairy that
Before you, you now see.

'If you will stay right by my side
And start your life anew,
My trusted servant fairies
Will all look after you.

'They'll wait upon you hand and foot –
Attend your every need,
The first one here is known as Moth
And this is Mustardseed.

'And here is lovely Peaseblossom,
And here is Cobweb too.
And they will take a special pride
In looking after you.'

Then turning to them all she said,
'You must do all you can
For my new love beside me here,
This handsome gentleman'

Titania then to Bottom said,
'Come over here my dear,
I have an overpowering wish
To kiss your hairy ear.'

But puzzled Bottom looked askance.
He didn't fancy this.
One thing he really didn't want
Was Queen Titania's kiss.

And so he looked away – ignored
Her every fervent plea,
And turning to the servants cried,
'Fairies! Attend to me!'

And then he told them bossily
Exactly what to do.
'Mustardseed, bring me some food –
And scratch me, one of you.'

And then he had a right old time
With other silly pranks,
And though they did all that he asked
He gave no word of thanks.

Then when he'd asked for everything
He ever had desired
He told the queen, 'I am replete
And now I'm feeling tired.'

She said, 'Of course you are my dear.
So lie upon my lap,
And close your eyes – relax awhile
And take a little nap.'

So lovingly she wrapped her arms
Around his hairy head.
'Sleep softly in my arms, my love,'
With tenderness she said.

And while he slept there peacefully
She sang a little song.
And at that very moment
King Oberon came along.

'What's all this?' he sternly asked.
'You most unfaithful lass.
I never thought to find you here
And cuddling with an ass.'

The queen went very red indeed
And acted very coy.
The king saw his advantage.
He said, 'I want that boy!'

The queen was cornered and she looked
All guiltily at him.
How could she now deny the king
And not allow his whim?

And so it doesn't take that much
To make a spot on guess,
That cornered as she was, she said
A disconcerted 'Yes!'

For she was most embarrassed
That Oberon had found,
His queen, his wife, with loving arms
Wrapped tenderly around…

An ass! For heavens sake – an ass!
So what then could she do?
She said, 'All right my husband dear.
I'll give the boy to you.'

Oberon was very pleased
Now that he'd got his way,
A bit unfairly too in truth
Some readers just might say.

But he was of a turn of mind
To call a final truce,
So hastily he took a phial
Of his new magic juice,

And turning to Titania,
He threw it in her eyes,
And in a moment he destroyed
Her loving, heavy sighs.

She said, 'My darling Oberon
I have been very crass,
However could I fall in love
And with that ugly ass?

'I've no idea what happened.
I've been a bit insane –
Oh, Oberon, please let us be
A couple once again.'

She showed the king sincere regret
And much heartfelt remorse,
So Oberon was quick to say,
'Why yes my dear, of course.'

And then with great dexterity
He raised the ass's head.
'We'll leave this fool to sleep awhile,'
He laughingly then said.

Then hand in hand they crept away
Without another word,
So softly did they leave the glade
That they walked off unheard.

And as they went the king did say,
'Titania – now wait,
And listen very carefully;
I'll bring you up to date.'

And so he told her everything,
All that had passed that night,
About the lovers and their tiffs
And all about their plight.

And then he led her gingerly
To where the lovers were,
Sleeping safe and sound beneath
An overhanging fir;

For Puck in all his artfulness
Most cleverly had got
The lovers – yes all four of them
Right to the selfsame spot.

Hermia was the first to wake.
She looked around and thought
The love of her Lysander
Had sadly fallen short.

Then he awoke and happily
Saw Hermia right there,
And straight away he spoke to her
With tender, loving care.

And as they spoke about events
That had occurred that night,
They very quickly realised
That things were now all right.

'We're still a couple – still in love –
So it does truly seem
That all was strange invention
And possibly a dream.'

Then Demetrius came round –
He suddenly awoke,
And the lovers present there
Saw right then, at a stroke...

That he was quite besotted,
For he soon made it plain
That he was desperately in love –
It drove him quite insane.

So, when Helena rubbed her eyes
And when she woke up too,
Demetrius beside her vowed,
'I'm still in love with you.'

He really was in love again –
Adored the girl once more,
In just exactly the same way
As he had felt before.

The purple juice had done the trick
And made his passion burn,
For it had righted everything
And made his love return.

And Helena was very pleased,
And grateful too to hear,
The loving words that he now mouthed,
Which sounded so sincere.

~ ~ ~

And as our little fairy tale
Now pretty well near ends,
We can confirm the four of them
Were once again good friends;

But then oh, horror – mayhem –
What a huge surprise,
In disbelief and agony
They rubbed their red-rimmed eyes.

For now right out of nowhere
Egeus had appeared;
It was the thing that Hermia
Had truly greatly feared.

He angrily – persistently –
Had searched the tangled wood,
Till finally Egeus had,
With sadness, understood…

That young Demetrius, his choice
Would never ever wed
His daughter, thus he spoke to her
And with forbearance said…

'I am amazed at all these things
The fickle fates have sent,
But I accept reluctantly,
And so I must consent...

'For you to marry whom you wish –
So be Lysander's wife.
Just go ahead and marry him
And fear not for your life.

'You may now wed your chosen beau,'
Stoically he said.
'In fact I think it's fair to say
All four of you can wed.'

So everything was settled
And ended very well,
And that is all there is to say –
There's nothing more to tell...

Except perhaps – this little tale
May very likely seem
As if it were a fantasy,
Itself a kind of dream;

And who can say with certainty,
For you may well be right,
A tangled, muddled lover's dream
On a midsummer's night.

Also by Richard Cuddington

SHAKESPEARE'S TRAGEDIES IN EASY READING VERSE

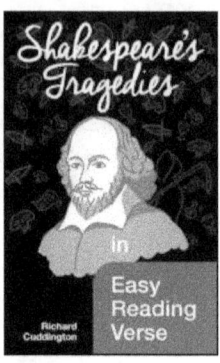

Richard Cuddington applies his Easy Reading Verse to Shakespeare's Tragedies. These are some of the Bard's most famous and compelling plays. Retold here in simple and engaging verse, the drama and excitement unfold with an urgency and momentum that captures the essence of the original plays.

Here the reader will meet Hamlet avenging his father's murder, Romeo risking all for his Juliet, Othello borne down with jealousy, Macbeth plotting to obtain Scotland's crown and many other colourful and doomed characters.

The sheer drama of some of Shakespeare's most memorable and highly acclaimed plays is captured here in fast moving, entertaining verse.

And when you know what each play is about you may well be encouraged to find out more about what makes these people tick by venturing into the original texts, having crept under the literary barrier and already found a way in by the back door.

SHAKESPEARE'S HISTORIES & ROMANCES IN EASY READING VERSE

Here in Richard Cuddington's Easy Reading Verse are Shakespeare's Histories and Romances which take the reader on two separate journeys. One through various turbulent periods of English history – the other through the slightly calmer waters of romance.

All the stories are told in clear and rhythmic verse which enhances the many dramatic and romantic situations. Readers will be entranced by the very diversity and richness of the colourful plots.

Here we meet Richard the Second losing his throne, Henry the Fifth conquering the French at Agincourt and Richard the Third using all his dastardly wiles to keep the crown. In contrast the Romances will introduce Prospero whipping up a tempest, Pericles losing, then finding his Thaisa and Palamon and Arcite fighting for the hand of Emilia. A veritable pageant of drama, turmoil and intrigue is encapsulated in these enthralling stories which are truly some of the Bard's finest plays.

These adaptations are an enjoyable and riveting read and act as an excellent bridge to the original texts.

SHAKESPEARE'S SONNETS IN EASY READING VERSE

Richard Cuddington's light-hearted adaptation of Shakespeare's Sonnets captures the essence of the original texts but in a way that makes them instantly accessible and understandable to the modern reader.

Originally published in 1609, many critics believe the Sonnets come closer to revealing Shakespeare the man, than any of his other works. Written in the first person, the Sonnets expose an emotional range that has given them enduring appeal.

The author now applies his straightforward Easy Reading Verse to create a fresh interpretation of the Sonnets. Here in simple and enjoyable lyrics, the mysteries of the Sonnets are unravelled, and with the original texts also contained within the book, they act as an aid in the understanding of Shakespeare's masterpieces.

CHAUCER'S CANTERBURY TALES IN EASY READING VERSE

For all its great reputation and the affection in which it is held, Chaucer's Canterbury Tales, written in 14th century Middle English, can actually be a daunting prospect to read. Richard Cuddington now steps in with a novel approach to Chaucer's famous gallery of pilgrims with their tales of chivalry, romance, courtly love, treachery, avarice, bawdiness, humour and nobility.

Whether you're new to the tales, or perhaps a teacher looking to enthuse and stimulate your students, or simply thinking of re-reading them, you will find here a thoroughly entertaining and immediately accessible way in to the storytelling genius of Chaucer in simple and amusing rhyming verse.

CHARLES DICKENS' OLIVER TWIST
IN EASY READING VERSE

Oliver Twist has been a family favourite ever since Charles Dickens gave birth to his marvellous story in 1837. It has been reproduced in many ways but now Richard Cuddington applies his Easy Reading Verse to recount this famous tale.

Here are all the familiar cast of characters – brought to life in fun, uplifting narrative verse that moves along at a vibrant pace. From the moment of Oliver's birth in the Workhouse, through all his adventures at the hands of Fagin and Bill Sikes until he finally finds a new life – there is never a dull moment.

The author has previously applied his straightforward, rhythmic style to The Complete Works of Shakespeare and Chaucer's Canterbury Tales and now turns to Dickens' famous story to retell it in a way that will have great appeal to children and adults alike.

CHARLES DICKENS' A CHRISTMAS CAROL IN EASY READING VERSE

Charles Dickens' A Christmas Carol is arguably the most dearly loved Christmas story ever written – a favourite with the whole family. Whether you are one of the many fans of the story or possibly even new to the tale – you will surely enjoy this adaptation, written in fast moving, light-hearted verse. Author Richard Cuddington, who has already adapted the complete works of Shakespeare and Chaucer's Canterbury Tales into fun filled, narrative verse, now applies his rhythmic style to this famous classic. Here is Scrooge in all his miserly misery, slowly being converted from his former monstrous self into a being who really knows how to celebrate Christmas. The charming verse takes us on an unstoppable journey where we meet the Spirits of Christmas Past, Present and Future, the joyful Mr. Fezziwig and of course, the tragic but lovable figure of Tiny Tim. And on the way Scrooge dominates a tale that celebrates the joy of Christmas, encouraging a belief that we should embrace its spirit throughout the year.

KENNETH GRAHAME'S THE WIND IN THE WILLOWS IN EASY READING VERSE

Here is a delightful re-telling of one of Britain's best-loved books, aimed at younger children but also providing a treat for Grahame's established legion of fans of all ages. Richard Cuddington's verse rendition of Kenneth Grahame's The Wind in the Willows is the perfect introduction to a volume of stories which have enchanted generations of readers with its timeless evocation of life 'along the river bank'. All the well-known characters are here: the Mole, the Water Rat, Badger, Otter and, of course, the larger-than-life and utterly irrepressible Mr Toad of Toad Hall. The author has retained all the verve and energy of the original tales, but simplified the language to make them more accessible to the younger reader. Mole's frightening visit to the Wild Wood in the depths of winter and the colourful adventures of Toad take centre stage in bubbling rhythmic verse that drives the ebullient narrative forward so that there is never a dull moment.

www.ingramcontent.com/pod-product-compliance
Lightning Source LLC
Chambersburg PA
CBHW071214080526
44587CB00013BA/1374